*What Every Child
Would Like
His Parents to Know*

Other Books by Dr. Lee Salk

The Psychology of Adjustment
How to Raise a Human Being
(with Rita Kramer)

What Every Child Would Like His Parents to Know[*]

by
Dr. Lee Salk

Director, Division of Pediatric Psychology
The New York Hospital-Cornell Medical Center

**To Help Him with the Emotional
Problems of His Everyday Life*

DAVID McKAY COMPANY, INC.
New York

Third Printing, April 1972

Designed by C. R. Bloodgood

Manufactured in the United States of America

To the memory of my parents,
Dora and Daniel Salk . . .
through their being, they left this world
a better place than when they entered it

Contents

What Every Child
Would Like
His Parents to Know

Chapter I

ᛜᛜᛜᛜᛜᛜᛜᛜᛜᛜᛜ

The Normal Emotional Problem

The rising concern of Americans about emotional health is real and justified. Most people are startled when I tell them that more than half the hospital beds in the entire United States at this very moment are occupied by people suffering from some form of mental disturbance. Emotional illness is devastating to the individual sufferers who are removed from the mainstream of their lives. Their families suffer, too. The disruption, the anguish, and the loss of individual human potential is heartrending.

The cost to society for the treatment and care of the emotionally disturbed is staggering. The number of trained professionals who should be employed to care for the emotionally sick and attempt to return them to normal life is enormous. The people already trained can make barely a dent in the existing problem. If every physician, psychiatrist, psychologist, social worker, and nurse in the United States today were diverted to dealing with emotional-health problems, they could not effectively help most of the people now suffering from emotional illness. There would not be enough of them, and the techniques they would have to use are overly time-consuming. And the human tragedy that results from those so deranged that they in some way traumatize others physically or mentally or commit acts of violence is hardly measurable. I know these are morbid facts, but they must be acknowledged so that one can focus on what should be done to help the growing number of people who are or will be afflicted with emotional problems.

The answer is prevention, eliminating the causes of emotional disturbances and preventing the occurrence of debilitating illnesses.

When I entered practice, I treated all sort of emotionally disturbed adults. What impressed me most was that no matter how hard I worked, no matter how hard the patient tried, the illness yielded terribly slowly, if at all. It was discouraging. I began to treat children, whose illnesses responded better to professional help. The chances of cure seemed better, and they indeed turned out to be.

Although the mental-health field is full of controversy, everyone apparently agrees that emotional problems are created very early in one's life and that abnormal patterns of behavior established at that time are extremely hard to reverse in adulthood. To make any modification is time-consuming and extraordinarily difficult. It is true that there can be change, but the possibility is limited. Even major psychotherapeutic treatment is frequently unsuccessful.

Clearly, if adult personality is markedly influenced by an individual's earliest experiences, we should concentrate preventive efforts on the very young. While most professionals in the mental-health field recognize this, relatively little effort is directed toward assisting those who are primarily responsible for the personality development of infants and young children—their parents. Over the past few decades, health services have grown so that prenatal care of pregnant mothers is accepted as routine. Well-baby care, including vaccinations and regular checkups by a pediatrician, is generally accepted because it has proved effective in preventing disease and in diagnosing illnesses that can be treated early, and therefore effectively. What shocks me is that so little emphasis has been placed on equivalent services to prevent and diagnose emotional health problems. For some strange reason, the only alternatives now available are either intensive psychotherapy or nothing at all. I fully expect that some day professionals will be trained, and they will be available to provide well-baby psychological care. But for the moment, parents must go it alone.

In my years of practice, I have found that many parents, who are indeed the first line of emotional care, are as misinformed as they are well-meaning. Too often they are innocent victims of old prejudices that linger on. They tend to follow the advice of others who seem to be better informed but who may, in fact, be equally misinformed. Since there is no one to help them and no reliable source of information, they must rely on their own wandering common sense. This book is meant to help parents apply the most advanced psychological theory in a commonsense manner toward easing their children's emotional problems.

Emotional problems are of varying magnitude. Some are usual everyday experiences, while others are reflections of a severe deep-rooted pathology. A normal emotional problem is a typical minor emotional crisis that almost everyone can expect to encounter. Successfully handled, the normal problem's resolution strengthens an individual. Improperly resolved, the normal problem becomes an abnormal problem. In my opinion, most parents go wrong—if they are going to do so—because they misinterpret what their child is thinking. Certainly they do not wish to harm their children. Hopefully, the knowledge presented in this book will give parents the information they need to cope with their child's everyday emotional confrontations.

Chapter II

〇〕〇〕〇〕〇〕〇〕〇〕〇〕〇〕〇〕〇〕〇〕〇

The Newborn Infant

*If I am nervous about caring for
my newborn baby, will that
harm him?*

It is perfectly normal and utterly natural for any parent to
be nervous about taking care of a newborn baby, particularly
if this is your first child. But the more time you spend caring
for your child from the very beginning, the more quickly
your confidence will grow. If you can work it out so that you
can care for him right in the hospital, you will gain confidence even before you get home.

Your nervousness is a trait that mothers of all living things
exhibit after giving birth, and is part of an instinctive protective concern. In the course of evolution, nature equipped
mothers with many natural drives and protective instincts in
order to ensure the survival of the species. So, some nervousness on your part, and your husband's, won't blunt your
effectiveness as parents. Anyway, there are normal genetic
and biological factors working on behalf of your baby's safe
passage into the world.

How do genetics and biology
affect my baby?

You inherit a desire and capacity to care for your offspring, a consequence of an intricate set of biochemical factors, developed in the course of evolution, which trigger built-in behavior patterns. Several animal investigations into the nature of maternal-infant relationships reveal much about mother instincts. When a baby lamb or kid is separated from its mother immediately after birth and kept away from her for as little as one hour, the mother seems to lose her capacity to differentiate her own young from others. Some studies have shown that she may even reject her offspring entirely. On the other hand, if mother and child stay together long enough for the mother to have a chance to lick her newborn, she will be able to identify it in a large flock, even after a long period of separation. Observations such as these suggest that directly after birth a critical period exists in which to establish a bond between mother and newborn. If this interval passes without the necessary contact between mother and child, the bond is weak. The young animal's chances of surviving to full maturity are lowered because the mother is less inclined to protect her young from predators and to teach it what it will need to know to survive.

After years of contact with hundreds of mothers in maternity wards, I have become convinced that the findings of these animal studies are not altogether unique to nonhuman animals. If they are not, then we should seriously question the wisdom of separating mothers from their babies immediately after delivery, a standard procedure in many hospitals. Human mothers and babies both show a need for mutual nearness and reciprocal stimulation. A mother is noticeably sensitive to the presence of her baby. She feels a rather strong and powerful desire to touch her baby, to hold him, and to talk to him. I have noticed that a mother almost always smiles back with great pleasure whenever her baby smiles at her.

Soon, the baby learns to take cues from her responses. In my opinion, the reciprocal interrelationship is the biologically natural course of events, which you do not have to create but with which you must not allow others, or even your own preoccupations, to interfere.

Then my child needs me?

In the early weeks and months of life your infant does need you, his mother, alertly sensitive to his cues and ever ready to respond to his needs. Love, care, handling, responsive faces, all are required for your child to be convinced that the environment reacts when he acts. Your natural biological tendencies, if they are not interfered with, will provide this kind of satisfaction for your baby with little effort on your part. The normal back-and-forth trading between mother and child across a whole spectrum of sensory experience cannot be substituted for in any way or made up for in later life. In order for it to occur with maximum effectiveness, you must be willing to follow your own nature. If you turn your back on the experience, you throw away one of the most profound and meaningful facets of all human experience. But your baby loses even more. He loses his chance to learn when he should be learning. Giving him twice what he needs later does not make up for what he needed earlier. He has grown beyond that stage and has already lost out. Watering a withered plant doesn't revitalize it.

When my child is born, to what extent does he see, hear, and feel?

An enormous amount of research information shows that newborn infants can see, hear, focus, and show preferences for various kinds of stimulation. All the newborn's senses are alive—sight, hearing, taste, smell, touch, movement. Within forty-eight hours after birth, newborn infants show a marked preference for more complicated visual stimuli. Moreover, they seem to prefer more complicated patterns in black and white, even if the less complicated patterns are in bright colors. Babies prefer their mother's rhythms in rocking them in preference to other rhythms. In studies I have conducted, newborn babies seem to cry less and be more content in the hospital nursery when exposed to certain sounds, such as a normal heartbeat sound. One of the most easily observed learning capacities in the human newborn is his ability to become accustomed to a repetitive stimulus. Studies have shown that newborn babies react differently to a new stimulus, but with continued exposure to the stimulation become familiar with it. If the initial stimulus is changed, even in the slightest manner, a newborn baby recognizes the difference. These studies indicate that babies quickly get used to a situation, become bored, and want some variation. Observations of this sort indicate a baby's capacity to differentiate sensations and demonstrate preferences. It also shows that from birth on, your baby is capable of learning. Incidentally, we know that early stimulation of the sensory apparatus in your baby's nervous system will, in later life, give him an increased capacity for learning.

Should I deliberately subject my child to stimulation?

Some parents have the idea that the newborn baby requires only food, sleep, and a dry diaper. This is not so. Your newborn infant arrives with five working senses: sight, hearing, taste, smell, and touch. He is also responsive to temperature differences, to pain, and to sensations of movement and changes in body position. He may also have other capacities that we do not entirely understand. But we do know that your baby has a strong need for stimulation and for having this stimulation vary from time to time. Babies are bored as easily as anyone.

Studies on human infants have shown that a baby who receives too little stimulation is likely to show little interest in exploring his environment and startles easily when presented with normal amounts of stimulation. On the other hand, babies who are "overloaded" with stimulation, that is, more than they are able to handle, are overwhelmed and frightened; these infants begin to avoid stimulation. What your baby requires is a moderate amount of stimulation, which facilitates exploratory behavior and at the same time helps establish a greater capacity for tolerating higher amounts of stimulation. Babies who do receive an appropriate amount of stimulation seem to learn more from the environment, retain more information, show a greater capacity to use it intelligently in problem-solving situations, and are better able to achieve their genetically determined intellectual potential than babies whose early stimulation was markedly diminished or overwhelming and frightening.

Where does my baby acquire
his need for sensory stimula-
tion?
Probably in the uterus before birth. As a pregnant mother moves about, motion is transmitted into the uterus and stimulates the baby's sense of movement through something in the baby's nervous system called the vestibular apparatus. There are kinesthetic and tactile stimulations in the uterus while your baby is growing, and there are sound stimuli— the mother's heartbeat and the noises of her digestion. A fetus will respond to sound stimuli provided externally. Incidentally, although any sense of visual sensation in the uterus is unlikely, we cannot rule out the possibility that it occurs. After all, even when our eyes are closed to variations in light, we still experience the sensation of vision—for example, during our dreams.
You will be interested to know that a baby who receives

considerable stimulation prenatally may very well have a greater need for stimulation after birth. Scientific observers have noted that a baby who was active as a fetus tends to be more active after birth. He will be a more alert baby. These facts lead me to conjecture that it might be advisable for mothers to continue their normal physical activity during pregnancy, provided it is not carried to such an extreme that it leads to premature labor or damage to the fetus. The mother who diminishes her activity during pregnancy, thinking this best, may inadvertently be diminishing stimulation for the growing fetus just at the time when normal activity might be more appropriate. One last point: while prenatal factors probably contribute to the level of your baby's need for sensory stimulation, the basic need is inherited. It developed in the course of evolution and has helped human beings to survive.

*How can I best fulfill my baby's
need for sensory stimulation?*

Initially, your newborn baby's need for sensory stimulation is satisfied primarily when he is being fed. Most newborn infants sleep for long periods and wake up around the time they need to eat. While feeding, for example, your baby is provided with visual stimulation by the movement of his mother's face and hands. Most newborn babies show a phenomenal tendency to look at the face and into the eyes of the person feeding them. Your baby's penetrating and exciting stare usually stimulates a smile and baby talk from the parent feeding him. Holding your baby in a relaxed manner during feeding provides him with pleasant tactile sensations. Most people feeding newborn babies tend to stroke them, touch them, and play with them. By means of these spontaneous movements and sounds, your baby receives a great deal of stimulation. Actually, all his senses are being employed simultaneously. He is getting a sense of taste, smell, touch, and movement, in addition to auditory and visual stimulation. If your baby's total sensory involvement is accompanied by pleasant relaxation, he feels secure and gratified. He will begin to look toward people for his satisfactions.

When a mother is tense and unhappy, her tension and unhappiness may be communicated to her infant during the feeding process. Her jerky and erratic movements can frighten the newborn, resulting in an irritable and uncomfortable baby. Needless to say, tension and discomfort during a baby's early feedings can interfere with his sense of security and his early emotional development. But do not confuse the feelings of tension and unhappiness I have just described with the feelings aroused by your inexperience. Nature takes care of them very soon. Even the most inexperienced mother, if she spends time at it, quickly adjusts to handling her baby, becoming more skillful and more at ease with her infant day by day.

Should I breast-feed my baby?

Every mother should give careful consideration to her feelings about breast-feeding. Free yourself from all the advice and stories other people have told you, and try to make your own decision based on your own feelings and perhaps those of your husband. If you want to breast-feed your child, by all means do so. If you do not, it would be best if you avoid becoming involved. What is most important is for you to feel happy about feeding your child. That you be confident and content is much more important to your infant than where the milk comes from. A mother who breast-feeds her child because she has been brainwashed into believing that her child will be disturbed if she does otherwise can consciously or unconsciously react so negatively to breast-feeding that she makes the feeding process uncomfortable for her child. The matter of whether to breast-feed or not really boils down to understanding what makes the feeding experience a satisfying one for your child. The answer is a contented mother. Respond to your own feelings so that the feeding relationship can be a pleasant one.

If you are indecisive or perhaps indifferent about breast-feeding, my feeling is to encourage breast-feeding, a natural process which should be encouraged on that basis alone. And there is another point to consider. Breast-feeding does tend to keep you within four or five hours of your infant, ensuring that you will have continued contact with your infant at relatively frequent intervals. The frequent contact between mother and child is important to the baby's healthy psychological growth because the natural physiological contacts that take place during breast-feeding ensure that the baby will have the sensory stimulation he needs for healthy emotional growth. The breast-feeding mother simply cannot avoid doing her part.

Why does my baby cry?

A baby's cry is an urgent signal of discomfort resulting from either physical or psychological factors. Usually the physical causes are hunger, a dirty or wet diaper, discomfort caused by heat or cold, physical pain caused by gastric upset, an open diaper pin, or other such factors. Many books discuss these problems. Much less recognized is the fact that a physically comfortable baby often cries because he is bored and requires some kind of sensory stimulation. It is just as important to provide your child with sensory stimulation to decrease his boredom as it is to meet his physical needs.

*What do I do to stop my baby's
crying?*

A crying infant is always unhappy. He is not, as the old story goes, exercising his lungs. What you must do is to try to make him happy. Go to him, find the cause of his discomfort, and correct it. Never let him "cry it out." This advice is

particularly important during the first nine or ten months
of your baby's life because it is then that your child develops
a lifetime sense of trust or distrust in people based upon his
experiences with the satisfaction people provide in response
to his pleas for help—his cries. If you respond, he learns
that people respond to one another, and he learns to trust
people to help him.

*If my baby is crying, should I
pick him up?*

Because of your infant's apparent satisfaction when he is
picked up and carried about, it is fair to conclude that he
probably has a need for being picked up. Being carried
about provides your baby with increased visual stimulation,
tactile stimulation through touch, and kinesthetic stimulation
through the sense of movement he gets in his muscles as he
clings to the person carrying him. Babies are pleased when
their senses are stimulated. Thus, you certainly should pick
up your baby if he cries for more than a few moments, like
when he is turning over in his sleep.

Studies have shown that if babies are picked up more
often, they cry less. The particular study I have in mind
started by finding out when babies tended to be fussiest
during the day. The pattern was noted, and the babies
studied were picked up for short periods just before they
were expected to cry. When they were picked up for these
short periods of time, they did not cry and fuss as much.
The conclusion must be that picking up and holding babies
satisfies their needs for stimulation, tends to offset the baby's
discomfort, and minimizes fussiness.

*Why not let my baby cry until
he stops?*

If you allow your baby to cry for a long period of time, he
eventually assumes that no help is forthcoming from others.

If this experience is repeated, and if the periods of frustrated crying are prolonged, a baby tends to turn to other means than people for the satisfaction of his needs. Babies who are left to cope with their own unhappiness often engage in self-stimulation, such as rocking back and forth or head-banging. They are inclined to go off to sleep in the course of their frustration. If sleep or self-stimulation helps the baby to reduce his discomfort, this behavior pattern is reinforced. The baby develops a tendency either to turn inward or to withdraw from reality. Understandably, he does not learn to turn to people for help. This pattern carried over into adulthood is a form of schizophrenia.

Sometimes when your baby cries, he seems to be reassured simply by seeing that someone is close by, a reaction that occurs sometime after the first six months of life. Although your baby initially needs the actual physical contact of being picked up to reassure him, and later the sight of you, after the first year of life when he begins to walk, he may not even need to have you in view all the time. He may simply need an occasional "fix"; which is why he may interrupt an activity and run to see if you are around before going back to what he was doing. The tendency of your child to give up the need for actual physical contact demonstrates an important principle. When a primitive need is satisfied, a child is able to take on the frustrations of the next stage in growth.

Pushing independence on a dependent newborn never works. Independence is learned only when the baby's dependency needs have been satisfied. Over and over again I hear parents and trained nurses state, "When a baby cries, he only wants to be picked up. Don't spoil him." They feel it is important to let a baby experience anxiety. So they let him cry to start him out "on the right foot." This does not work. True, frustration often fosters learning, but one has to take into consideration the intensity of the frustration, the capacity of the individual, and the context in which the frustration occurs. Excessive frustration does not foster learn-ing. So while they think they are teaching frustration toler-ance in early infancy, the infant may be learning that his parents cannot be trusted to help. It is far more sensible to help your infant overcome his difficulties during this early period of great dependency by meeting his needs directly. Later, as your child grows and shows increased capacity for dealing with frustration, you can teach him to use his own capacities to solve problems.

But won't trying to keep my
baby constantly happy spoil
him?

Actually the concept of "spoiling" is not very clear. When I have asked people to define spoiling, they are hard put to find an adequate definition. When they talk about a spoiled child, they generally mean that the child is demanding and unable to put off gratification; they usually mean one who has temper tantrums when he doesn't get his way, one who is never satisfied.

I myself feel it is impossible to spoil an infant. The concept of spoiling just does not apply to babies under the age of nine or ten months, since they are utterly dependent, com-pletely incapable of satisfying their own needs, and abso-lutely unable to put off any gratification without some sense of frustration. They require the cooperation of adults to be satisfied. You won't spoil your baby by helping him. As a matter of fact, if you force frustration on your infant by not meeting his primitive needs, there is a greater chance that he will cling to his infantile behavior than if you satisfy these needs quickly and with little frustration. Believe me, his capacity for independence will flourish and grow if he has had a gratifying life during his early infancy.

Chapter III

⊙⫯⊙⫯⊙⫯⊙⫯⊙⫯⊙⫯⊙⫯⊙⫯⊙⫯⊙⫯⊙⫯⊙

Who Takes Care of
Your Child?

*Who is the best person to care
for my child?*

The best person to care for any child is his parent. Regardless of how well trained or how well-meaning other people may be, they are not likely to have the deep attachment you have for your own children. The protective feelings that biological parents have for their children are essential for the propagation of the species. Undoubtedly they have been crucial to the survival of the human race. Imagine what it would be like if parents did not have these feelings.

A parent's "drive" toward parenthood is a rather strong biological complex that shows itself in interplay whereby parents' behavior affects their child, and the child's behavior in turn affects the parents. As the child is more responsive, his parent becomes more involved in the child's activities. The excitement a parent shows when a child smiles for the first time conveys something back to the child that reinforces the use of smiling to elicit a reaction from his parent. By means of this reciprocal interplay, parents communicate their values and their feelings, and pass on their own knowledge to the next generation. There is no question about this process when day after day one observes new mothers with their

17

new babies. Their feelings of delight and pride in conjunction with their tenderness and overwhelming desire to care for their children attest to this mystery.

Have you ever observed that the deep emotional attachment between parent and offspring in most mammalian species is heartwarming to most people for one reason or another? Perhaps seeing the attachment elicits a special kind of satisfaction as we remember the feelings of safety we had in the presence of our parents. All other things being equal, the biological connection between a parent and his child enhances communication and makes him especially geared to the job of caring for his own child.

How does biology enter into
my relationship with my child?

Many hormone changes take place during pregnancy, during childbirth, and immediately after birth. These changes last afterwards for a period of three to four weeks. They are an integral part of the childbirth process and specifically prepare a mother for receiving her new child. One hormone change, for example, facilitates the flow of milk, which in turn facilitates feeding, handling, and protecting the new offspring.

As I noted earlier, numerous animal studies have shown that separation of mothers from their offspring interferes with the mother's development of the maternal response that creates the best possible environment for growth of the offspring. I have found in some of my own studies that prolonged separation between a mother and her child following birth causes some changes in the way the mother holds her new child. Perhaps the biological relationship is interfered with. In any case, all the studies support the idea that a mother should care for her own child as soon as possible following the birth of the child. Delay between delivery and the assumption of child-caring activities should be minimized.

Is there a biological factor in
my child's relationship with his
father?

Yes, there is, because your child bears a genetic relationship to his father and has temperamental features and various other factors attuned to the father's own temperament and personality. These similarities facilitate communication through interplay. A father's pride in his child's accomplishments and his wish to have a "chip off the old block" suggest a biological factor. Most fathers wish to have a child that carries on into the next generation some of his own characteristics. Perhaps this is the reason why most fathers, whether they admit it or not, want a son for their first child. I would even go so far as to say that most fathers have a secret desire to bear a child themselves. I hasten to add that this desire is very deep-rooted and manifests itself in various forms of behavior that only the psychoanalyst recognizes as indicative of a deep-rooted desire. For example, many men refer to a new project as "a pregnant idea." A successfully completed piece of work in which a man takes pride is called "my baby." While many people will regard these observations as foolishness, this kind of analysis has contributed to our knowledge about human development.

Should a father change diapers
and feed his child?

Absolutely and without question. The father should take care of his baby, and he should be involved from the beginning, perhaps even before the baby is born. I have noticed over and over again that fathers who have participated with their wives in preparation for parenthood seem unusually close to their children, particularly when they have decided upon natural childbirth and the father has helped directly in the delivery. These fathers are closer to their wives and seem much more demonstrative in their expressions of love for their children. In my experience they enjoy fatherhood more and find it extremely pleasurable.

Our culture has placed too little emphasis on a father's caring for his child. In many ways we have fostered attitudes that deprive fathers of the pleasures of parenthood. The attitude that gets passed from generation to generation assigns the father a role primarily concerned with paying bills and doling out discipline. It would be far better for future generations if this attitude could be changed so that a father's role in child care could be looked upon with esteem. Not only would it be helpful to each individual child, but the attitude would be passed on to subsequent generations so that what we now recognize as the father's role would be more properly geared to the needs of our children.

Incidentally, I think a father's involvement is very important not only for the emotional well-being of the child but also for the mother herself, who does appreciate a husband who assists her. The marital sense of cooperation is enhanced, and the mother tends to feel less resentment about the tedious aspects of child-rearing.

Will it harm my child if I leave
him with someone else?

No, it won't if the person with whom you leave your child is responsible and will care for your child's emotional needs and his needs for stimulation as well as his physical health. I think it is absolutely essential for you to spend some time away from your child now and again. It is also good for your child to be with other people from time to time. How good this separation is for your child depends largely on his age and how long you are to be gone, who takes care of your child, and what his reactions are to the caretaker.

*How will I know who is a
proper caretaker for my child?*

Almost anyone can take care of your baby's physical needs. His emotional needs are the ones with which I am most concerned, since these have the greatest effect on his growing personality. Needless to say, the people who are chosen to take care of babies and young children should be warm, understanding, well adjusted, and above all, they should enjoy children. It is far easier to enumerate these qualities than to define what they are. Perhaps I can suggest what you should avoid. Watch out for people who are overly concerned with neatness and cleanliness, since they generally put those interests before the emotional needs of your child. People who are inclined to dominate you would probably undermine the relationship between you and your child. People who are depressed or who have some personality characteristic that keeps them from being lighthearted and spontaneous might be unable to give your growing child the kind of stimulation he needs. Often a person promoted as a well-trained, well-experienced, and knowledgeable baby nurse may not necessarily be the person best equipped to care for your child.

I think it is most helpful to rely on your instincts in choosing someone to care for your child in your absence. Generally speaking, mothers who are primarily concerned with their babies care during the first few months of the baby's life and who develop a sensitivity to the needs of their babies seem to have good sense about selecting people to take care of their children. This same sensitivity will help them judge correctly when and for how long they can leave their children with other people. You can usually almost "feel" whether a given person will be able to care for your child in a way that makes the child feel secure and comfortable. The most crucial point to consider is how your child feels about that person. Children generally like people who enjoy them and dislike those who don't. No matter how qualified the person may be, if your child is fearful or anxious, or if you feel somewhat apprehensive about the person's sensitivity to your child, respect this feeling and act upon it.

Does my child distinguish between its parents and a caretaker?

Yes. There is good reason to believe that your child becomes accustomed to the way you handle him and feed him, the way you sound, and perhaps even the way you smell. He begins very early in life to distinguish his parents from other people, recognizing the difference somewhere around the fourth or fifth month of life, although some children don't show this capacity until a month or two later.

Unfortunately, it is possible for you to blur the distinction if you do not assume the primary responsibility for your child's care and are inclined to spend long periods of time away from him. If you have numerous caretakers for your child, selected without care and without any particular consistency, your child will be less inclined to see you as special. To allow this to happen is a great mistake. It is extremely important for any child to know his own parents, because the depth of the relationship between parent and child very early in life is the prototype for that child's relationships with other people later on. Children who have been passed from person to person and have not gotten to know their own parents, as they grow older, frequently show difficulties in establishing close and meaningful relationships with other people.

Will a long separation damage
the relationship between me
and my child?

This question is hard to answer, since it is difficult to know what might have happened had the separation not taken place. Separation experiences do have a different effect on children at different stages in their development. However, research has shown that a separation of even one night during the first two years of a child's life tends to contribute to an increased number of problems with subsequent separations. Some doctors who work with children even feel that a separation at this early age may cause sleep disturbances.

Most people think that it does no harm to go away and leave a very young child, because they feel the baby does not know the difference. This is not true. In fact, the opposite is true. The very young child does know, vividly. Because he has very little concept of "now" and "later," a baby does not understand that if you go away you will ultimately come back. Any baby generally assumes that if he cannot see you, you are no longer there; in fact, you don't even exist. His reaction is based solely on whether or not he sees you.

You cannot prepare your child for a separation until he has acquired the concept of time, that is, until he understands the idea of something happening now and something happening later on, or something happening today and something happening tomorrow. Until your child understands that concept, even a one-day separation experience can have bad results. Your child cannot help but anticipate any parting experience as one leading to prolonged separation. Prolonged separation always frightens a young child, since it means that you no longer exist, and the concept of a parent not existing arouses a great deal of anxiety. Thus your child experiences acute anxiety every time you leave him, whether or not you are going for any length of time.

Do you mean I should never
leave my baby?

No. It's important to feel free enough to go shopping, visit friends, and handle similar matters away from home. But don't overdo it. The point I want to make is that your baby becomes attached to you and misses you when you are not there. Some babies, cared for by others from the start, don't attach themselves strongly enough to their parents to care whether their parents are or are not with them. While this might be convenient for a mother who wants more "freedom," she is in a sense preventing her child from establishing a close tie to his mother.

Strangely enough, one of the ways we know about separation anxiety in children involves playing "peek-a-boo." I'm sure you have had the pleasure of playing peek-a-boo with a baby. The enormous pleasure and giggling that you see in a young child when you play peek-a-boo stems from the reduction in his anxiety that he feels when he no longer sees you. If you play peek-a-boo, meaning that he doesn't see you and then all of a sudden he does, and your child giggles, it means that he did not expect you to be there, and then all of a sudden there you were. Slowly he learns that you are there even when he doesn't see you. He is happier and less anxious when he is reassured that not seeing you does not necessarily mean you no longer exist.

Needless to say, it is easier for me to recommend that you do not engage in any activities that will cause a premature separation between you and your child than it is for you to follow the recommendation. What you do is up to you, but whatever you do, you should know what's going on in your child's mind.

How do I prepare my child for
a necessary separation?

Because your child needs to maintain continuity in his relationship with you, it is probably best that he remain at home when you go away. Moreover, it will be best if he is in the care of someone whom he has known and with whom he feels secure. Preferably, that person should be someone who has spent considerable time with you and your child in your home. If you have to leave your child and place him in someone else's home, the unfamiliarity might arouse additional anxiety about the separation experience. It is hard for me to advise in a hard and fast way what you should do, because of all the possible combinations and permutations. For example, your child might feel more comfortable in the home of someone he knows and feels secure with than in his own home in the care of someone who is new to him.

If your child grasps verbal communication and understands that you are going away, you can prepare him for the separation simply by explaining in advance, perhaps one week or so, about your anticipated trip. Explain in detail who will take care of him, when you will return, and other concrete factors that will describe the subsequent event. Obviously, if your child likes the person with whom you leave him, the separation experience will not be too traumatic and perhaps can even be enjoyable. On the other hand, no matter how much you prepare your child in advance, if the person he is left with is someone he doesn't enjoy, someone insensitive to your child's needs, nothing will take away your child's discomfort.

Should I take my child with me if I can?

Yes. It is advisable for you to take your child with you as much as you can. If children accompany their parents at very early ages, even in infancy, they become accustomed to new sights, new sounds, and new places. Since even very young children are able to adapt to varying levels of stimulation, a child who gets a great deal of exposure to different environmental conditions, will be more adaptable later on. Most of us know that a child who has slept only in a quiet room wakes very easily at the slightest sound. So taking your child with you not only diminishes his anxiety when you leave him behind, but the trip itself can serve as a very rewarding experience for the child.

However, if you take your child on a trip and then in a strange environment engage strange people to watch him in a strange hotel room as you disappear to go sightseeing, the experience could be more devastating than leaving your child at home with a familiar person. Ideally, when you are on a trip and plan to spend some time away from your child, you should take pains to have your child well familiarized with his new environment and the new person before you leave him. What I am saying may sound confusing and inconsistent, but I am trying to emphasize that taking your child on a trip can be a most rewarding experience or a most frightening experience. Recognize the importance of giving your child time to adapt to a new place and new people before you go off for an evening.

What about baby-sitters?

It is strange that many people are much more careful in selecting people to care for their automobiles than they are in choosing people to care for their children. This irresponsibility is particularly distressing, since the future of our civilization depends largely on future generations, and future generations will be markedly influenced by the way we handle them in early infancy and childhood. In spite of the fact that many people think that the selection of baby-sitters is not an important task, let me emphasize that it is. Baby-sitting should not be assigned to just anyone available to be in physical proximity with your child. Some baby-sitters are wonderful with children, but some baby-sitters totally lack any understanding of your child's needs. They spend little time with him, disregarding his cries, to say nothing of his desires to play and be cared for in an attentive way. Incidentally, if your child becomes frightened with a particular baby-sitter and if you go off and leave your child with this person again, it is reasonable to expect that your child will remain frightened. When you suspect something frightening has happened, do not re-engage that baby-sitter.

How should I arrange for a
baby-sitter for my child?

After picking a person who you know likes children and is sensitive to their emotional needs, you should arrange to have the chosen baby-sitter come to your home a while before you plan to leave. Your child needs between a half-hour and an hour to become accustomed to a new person. Try to have familiar people as baby-sitters. If you can't, make some attempt to have your child experience some positive interaction between his parents and the new baby-sitter. As a general principle, it is best for your child to meet strangers in your presence, if for no other reason than that you can offer reassurance if your child reacts to the stranger fearfully. Remember that children often establish their attitudes about people by using their parents' responses as guides. If it becomes apparent that the baby-sitter is a friendly person acceptable to you, your child will most likely accept the baby-sitter, too.

Some parents are inclined to short-circuit proper introductions. They get all ready to leave. As soon as the baby-sitter comes, whether or not their child is familiar with that person, they immediately depart, leaving the baby-sitter to cope with their child's anxiety. This common procedure is a most traumatic experience for your child and can make it extremely difficult for him to accept amiably subsequent departures. Worse yet, many parents think it is advisable to put a child to bed before the baby-sitter comes, so that the child will not even know that his parents have gone. This procedure is highly inadvisable. If your child awakens before your return to find a strange someone he does not know, his reaction can only be one of dismay, perhaps horror. After all, if your child goes off to sleep and wakes up to find a stranger in your place, he may associate going off to sleep with losing you and finding a stranger in your place. Needless to say, this experience can cause any child to be reluctant to go to sleep. Not only is this childish reaction logical and sensible, it is amply confirmed by clinical experience.

Do you favor day-care centers for children?

Day-care centers have their good points and their bad points. Day-care centers provide care for children while their mothers for one reason or another are away. They provide social stimulation, group play, and initial learning activities. In many instances a child would not have these experiences even if his mother had the time available to take care of him herself. Obviously, some care is better than none at all. But you should recognize that the people who are employed by a day-care center to care for children are not necessarily capable.

I have often found that parents assume that people at a center would not be employed there unless they were highly qualified, more so than the parent. Since this is not always true, always retain the primary responsibility for your child. The day-care center should not replace the family.

Incidentally, a day-care center can serve a very useful purpose apart from caring for and stimulating a child in his everyday life. There are many children whose mothers are extremely cautious and who warn their children of all kinds of disasters that might occur, such as falling off the swing, tripping when running, and so on. A mother who tends to be overprotective in this way can inhibit her child's curiosity about the way the world works. A day-care center can help free a child like this. And children who feel lonely because their parents tend to be indifferent may enjoy a day-care center that provides social stimulation.

Can a mother work and be a
good parent?

Yes, but generally speaking if a mother does not have to work, if she has a husband to support her, or if she has saved for the birth of her child, she shouldn't, for at least the first nine or ten months of her baby's life. It benefits both mother and child if, during this period, the mother assumes the role of primary caretaker for her child. As everyone knows, it's a big job to care for a baby, and it's a full-time job for all but a few exceptional mothers.

I feel quite strongly that spending full time with your baby in these early days, weeks, and months, and considerable amounts of time thereafter until, say, your child is ready to go to school, is an investment in your child's emotional development that will pay handsome dividends later. Your child will have an increased capacity to withstand stress and will know how to establish warm and close relationships with other people. The freedom that you give up when your child is young will be more than returned to you later, because your child will be more independent, more stable, and more able to function on his own. The attention you withhold from a young child will be demanded doubly when he is older.

How soon a mother should go back to work depends on the job she does, where she does it, who takes care of her child while she's at work, how time-consuming her work is, and whether she can arrange a schedule that permits her to fulfill her responsibilities as mother.

Is there a preferable way for a
working mother to arrange her
schedule?

A working mother should attempt to arrange her work schedule so that she can return home in the middle of the day, perhaps to eat with her young child until the child is at least two and a half or three years of age. It is important to arrange frequent contacts at shorter intervals than an all-day span. Such a schedule makes your child's separation from you far less disturbing to him. Actually, even a young child can make do with less total time with his parents if the intervals of separation are not prolonged.

Recently a research technician in a laboratory at the hospital where I work asked me if I thought it would be advisable for her to work three days a week, now that her child was nine months old. She planned to work three days a week and spend the remaining four with her child. I suggested to her that she might find it more enjoyable and that it might also be better for her child if she worked five days a week, but arranged to spend a long block of time in the middle of the day with her child. Such a schedule would give her an opportunity to see her child and feed him, and it would also give her a schedule that she liked better, since it represented working full time.

I feel quite strongly that business and government organizations should accommodate themselves to mothers who must work. I see no reason why they cannot offer substantial time during the middle of the day to help the mother assume her family responsibilities. Strangely enough, most businesses and government organizations pay little attention to any worker's family responsibilities. Men are sent on extended business trips. Families are uprooted and moved to different parts of the country without considering the problems of family adjustment. I know it would be healthier emotionally for a family, and I think it would minimize resignations and labor turnover, if industry would focus more on family needs. For example, business should not only finance an employee's lengthy business trip, but allow him to take his family along at company expense.

Incidentally, children who have working mothers often learn that they can exert a certain amount of control by becoming ill. No working mother puts her job before her child's illness. For this reason, a child may learn to develop secondary physical symptoms in response to his wish to have his mother take care of him. While this is understandable in terms of the child's psychological needs, it creates havoc with a responsible mother who not only wants to work but may need to work in order to maintain her family responsibilities. If this situation occurs, I think it important that the mother give priority to her relationship with her child, even if it requires her having to take a leave of absence.

If a mother must work, who should replace her?

No one. Someone can care for your child, but no one can replace his mother. A mother's work need not be detrimental to her child, provided it doesn't interfere with her role as mother. The free-lance researcher, the handicraft worker, anyone who works at home, can arrange her schedule comparatively easily in order to be able to spend time with her child and supervise his care. Others who go to offices may be able to organize a day that includes large segments of time for a child. Unfortunately, some mothers must work full time to support their families. Each of these mothers should apply her instincts and sensitivity to selecting the person she chooses to care for her child. And each must assume the primary responsibility for her child's care. If she makes the decisions about her child's care, no matter who actually cares for the child, she is assuming, as she should, the primary role.

Should a father be involved in
caring for children?

Yes. It is strange how little real attention is paid to the role of the father in the enormous number of books written on child care. In a sense, fathers have been ignored. And they have been pressured into accepting a somewhat limited role as a parent. Any father who limits himself to the position of the family disciplinarian and the family financial authority is missing out.

I feel quite strongly that fatherhood has many rewards and satisfactions that are unique. Fatherhood is just as pleasant as motherhood. Fatherhood represents an enormous achievement, one of the most marvelous experiences in life: the creation of another human being. It provides an opportunity to influence the development of a new life, to protect it, and to help it establish a position in society. One of the great pleasures you have as a father is the admiration and love your child gives you.

Many fathers find the direct emotional gratification they receive from their children's responses is only one of the many advantages of being a father. Fatherhood gives a man the opportunity to recapture many of the joys had in his own childhood. We ought to thank our children at times for giving us the opportunity to experience the many pleasures that come with parenthood. And I am concerned from time to time about why some fathers are not getting the most out of fatherhood.

The answer, I feel, lies in the fact that our culture has tended to deemphasize fatherhood while emphasizing other accomplishments. I think it's time that we place more emphasis on the importance of fatherhood and begin to concern ourselves with father love as well as mother love. Children enjoy the kisses, the affection, and the cuddling they receive from their fathers, but do you find this enjoyment appearing in an advertisement or in a TV commercial? In short, our society supports the idea of masculinity in a way that does not include child-care functions. Being a father who takes care of children and being masculine are not inconsistent. A father should be "loving and giving" in the care of his children. I feel that a good father is a little bit like a mother.

For obvious reasons, fathers are generally not able to spend as much time with their children as mothers are. The infrequency of an event shared by a child with his father does not detract from its importance. It may, in fact, enhance it. Incidentally, a child gets a certain sense of satisfaction out of being alone with his father. All too often a well-meaning father gathers all of his children together and plans a group excursion. While this can be enjoyable and rewarding, I think you should recognize that each child also needs to get to know each of his parents alone.

What are the possible effects of
not having a father around?

Scientific research on father deprivation helps answer this question. These studies make it quite clear that a father's handling of discipline and his ability to be not only strong but tender are the keys to his influence on his child's developing personality. The general feeling is that the father plays an important role in the development of his child's sexual identification and in his child's growth of a sense of right and wrong. Of course, not having a father around also deprives the child of many pleasurable experiences.

Research conducted on children whose fathers were away in the military service revealed that the boys in the group had a more "feminine orientation" than children whose fathers were at home. This feminine orientation seemed to persist even after the father returned. Moreover, boys whose fathers were absent during the first year of life seemed to have had more behavior difficulties than would normally have been expected. They seemed to have had more trouble establishing and keeping good relationships, not only with adults but with other children.

Other studies showed a reasonably clear relationship between delinquent behavior in boys and the absence of an adequate father (male) figure during childhood. Incidentally, the father might have been absent, or he might have been present but generally weak or ineffectual. This statement emphasizes that the physical absence of the father is not the only crucial factor. Having a father around who is weak and who does not take responsibilities with his child can sometimes be worse than having no father. After all, if someone takes the role but does not play the part adequately, it prevents someone else from filling the role and perhaps doing a better job.

What special knowledge will my child gain from his relationship with his father?

Fathers have a great deal of knowledge to give their children. To begin with, they transmit their knowledge about life directly. They teach values. His father's relationship with his mother offers the child the chance to observe all aspects of behaving like a husband. In addition, your child experiences his father's relationship with siblings. In families in which the father takes an active role in child care, the boys tend to help care for their siblings and act as parent surrogates when the need arises. Incidentally, a child watches very carefully the way in which his father reacts to the child himself. In this context, your boy learns how to be a father from his own father. A girl learns what a man is like and how a father behaves. What she learns about men helps her develop her own identification as a female, particularly if she has the experience of seeing her father with her mother.

As we look back upon our own experiences, we are invariably influenced not only by what we have experienced in our relationships with our own fathers, but also by what we have lacked in this relationship. I have known many people whose own fathers spent little time with them who have learned the importance of a father's relationship with his child. They develop a deep sensitivity for a child's own need for paternal interest and time.

Chapter IV

❖❧❖❧❖❧❖❧❖❧❖❧❖❧❖❧❖

Weaning Your Child

*Why is weaning important to
my child's emotional development?*

Because weaning is one of your child's first steps to independence. Prior to weaning, your infant is relatively passive
and dependent on others for the satisfaction of his needs. In
particular, he is absolutely dependent on you to bring him
the breast or a bottle. If you don't bring him food, he starves,
since he cannot move around to find food. As your child
grows, he begins to reach for objects and transfer them from
one hand to the other. He starts to move around in his
environment. He shows his ability to assert himself, and he
begins to demonstrate the continuing need to function with
increasing independence. Weaning specifically represents a
first step in your child's learning to be independent in satisfying his need for food and the concurrent need for sucking
satisfaction.

You should realize that the sucking response represents
the most highly developed function in the newborn infant.
An infant has a need to suck and remains tense until this
need is satisfied. A baby will even cry when he feels the
need to suck. Usually, because it is natural, a mother takes

care of the sucking needs by feeding her child. During either breast-feeding or bottle-feeding, the sucking needs and the nutrient needs are satisfied simultaneously. Thus, your baby begins to associate the feeding process with the gratification of his sucking response.

Weaning has emotional overtones because you can frustrate your child's sucking need at the time you are teaching your child to feed himself without your help. Weaning can be achieved satisfactorily only if your child's sucking need is satisfied while he is learning to hold a cup and bring food to his mouth himself.

Is sucking instinctive?

Infants are born with a sucking reflex. There's no question that a newborn infant initially establishes his contact with the world through his mouth. You don't have to attribute this concept to followers of Freud, Rank, or Erikson. All you have to do is observe young infants to be convinced. If you put your finger in the mouth of a newborn (please, first wash your hands thoroughly), you will find a rather substantial sucking grasp and surprisingly strong sucking movements. And since the newborn infant begins sucking almost as soon as an object is placed in his mouth and before this response has been reinforced, you can assume that sucking is an instinctive quality. There is even evidence that the need to suck existed before birth. Many babies are born with calluses on their thumbs. They have, perhaps by accident, gotten their thumbs in their mouths while they were in the uterus. This supposition is confirmed by photographs of fetuses showing thumb-sucking.

What is the purpose of my baby's sucking instinct?

Your child's sucking instinct facilitates contact between him and another object, particularly the natural object from which he receives food, the nipple. Babies who have poor sucking reflexes at birth have problems satisfying their nutritional needs. Other natural reflexes occur at the same time as the sucking reflex. If by chance your baby's hand is close enough to his face to touch his cheek, the touch causes the infant to open his mouth, grasp the hand, and engage in vigorous sucking. This example shows the sucking reflex operating together with another reflex that we call the rooting response. You have probably noticed that if you touch a young baby's face somewhere near his mouth, he tends to move in the direction of the touch. You can also observe the rooting response in action when a parent tries to move a baby's head by pushing it in a given direction. You will find that the baby opposes these movements and tends to move in the direction closest to the parent's touch. These sucking, and rooting reflexes probably provide the rudimentary behavior patterns that lead a child to a source of food and thus help provide sufficient nutrition for survival. In this way these reflexes have contributed to the survival of the species.

What is the relationship between sucking and feeding?

Initially your baby is motivated by the need to satisfy his sucking response, which later becomes associated with eating. At first, the sucking response is dominant. Some babies who have received enough food to leave them gorged seem to have a continuing need for sucking. While there seems to be no predetermined relationship between sucking and feeding in the very early days of life, my own experience tells me that sucking satisfaction should become associated with the intake of food. Ideally, your baby's need for sucking should be approximately equivalent to his need for food. That is, around the time he has received an adequate amount of food, sucking satisfaction should be complete. If your child is gorged and still seems tense and uncomfortable, or wants more to eat, it usually signifies that his sucking needs have not been met. If he shows a strong need for sucking by putting his hands in his mouth or by demonstrating a continued need for food after he is completely full, you might use a bottle nipple with a smaller hole to make your infant have to suck more to get the same quantity of food. If his mother breast-feeds him, you might let the child feed on only one breast at each feeding. The mother can reduce her own discomfort by pumping the other breast.

Take your cues from the behavior of your infant. When he has achieved sucking satisfaction, it is quite obvious. No technical knowledge or training is required to recognize this. The satiated infant, who just a moment ago sucked vigorously at the nipple, relaxes all his muscles, closes his eyes, retracts his facial muscles—which releases him from the nipple—smiles, and goes off to sleep. The unsatisfied infant is equally recognizable; he is tense, cranky, irritable, frustrated, and unable to relax. Often this baby will regurgitate and crave still more food in spite of the fact that he has already consumed more than he needs.

Is there any harm in using a pacifier?

While I am inclined to avoid using a pacifier, I am not absolutely opposed. When your child is in the hospital or ill or suffering in some other way, a pacifier could be very reassuring. But it is wrong to put a pacifier into a child's mouth the instant he cries. Recent research has shown that babies show less exploratory visual behavior while sucking on a pacifier than they would if a pacifier were not available. Since an infant learns a great deal about his environment by visual exploration, you can safely assume that a pacifier cuts down the external information your baby receives and interferes with the development of his thinking. Because your child has a need to be picked up and to move around, giving him a pacifier every time he is uncomfortable tends to reinforce the use of some kind of oral stimulation in place of other kinds of stimulation your infant needs. Giving an infant a pacifier every time he cries is not unlike giving an adult a tranquilizer every time he feels unhappy. It is far better to help your infant by finding out what is causing him to cry than to increase the use of the sucking response as the means for reducing anxiety.

Why does my child suck his thumb, his clothing, a toy, or any old thing?

The reason is simple. He has a need for sucking satisfaction that has not been met in conjunction with being fed. His sucking instinct was not sufficiently gratified so that he could relax in the consummation of his need.

Incidentally, if your baby continually sucks his thumb, it will not help much to take it out of his mouth time after time. Chance alone probably caused him to find his hand or thumb to achieve sucking satisfaction. The infant might have been put in his crib at bedtime and when his hand or thumb was inadvertently placed in his mouth this stimulated the rooting response which initiated the sucking response. His sucking response provided some gratification that reinforced the pattern and increased the likelihood that he would suck his thumb again.

While I do not recommend repeatedly stopping your infant's thumb-sucking, I do feel you can take your baby's hand from his mouth when you find him sucking his thumb as he goes to sleep. It also helps to make some attempt to relax him by rocking him, holding him, or simply being present. These variations will help your baby relax without sucking his thumb.

Will my child be permanently
affected by frustration of his
sucking needs?

I want to emphasize that frustrating your baby's need for sucking does not teach him to give up his desire for sucking. Satisfying the need does. After all, when you are hungry, there is nothing like a good meal to take away the hunger. For some strange reason, we are inclined to think that satisfying a child's need only prolongs it, when actually the opposite is true. The need persists, and a great deal of psychic energy focuses on various attempts to satisfy it. Improperly weaning your child can indeed be a severe cause of frustration with long-range effects. Interestingly, many mental-health experts contend that excessive drinking, smoking, and other oral indulgences are related to frustration at the time of weaning.

When, then, is the best time for
me to wean my child from the
breast or bottle?

The best answer to this question is probably an indefinite one. Because of individual differences, some babies can be weaned when they are close to one year of age; others may require a bottle until they are three, or, in some instances, even older. Other circumstances, such as stress in the family, or the birth of a sibling, may increase a baby's need for sucking satisfaction. Many pediatricians recommend weaning a child around the time he begins to teeth. In my opinion, this is an irrelevant indicator. The presence of teeth does not affect the need for sucking. In addition, it is a premature indicator, since most babies begin to get their teeth around the age of six to eight months, far too soon to begin weaning a baby. Since the primary task for a baby in the first year of his life is to develop a sense of trust, and since you will be minimizing frustration during this time, avoid frustrating your baby's need for sucking satisfaction. Don't try to wean him completely in his first year. Wait well beyond the first year, and begin slowly, while you're teaching your child to feed himself.

How should I wean my child?

Gradually. Ideally you should show your child how to use a cup somewhere around four, five, or six months of age. Do this while your child is still sucking on the breast or having a bottle. What you are doing is teaching your child two different ways for taking food. If you allow your child the sucking gratification of feeding from the breast or bottle while at the same time teaching him to drink from a cup, you will make total weaning less traumatic. At all costs, do not make an abrupt transition that will be doubly difficult for your child. The parent who decides that at a predetermined moment his child must give up the nipple and take on the difficult task of drinking from a cup frustrates the infant. The double difficulty is that his frustration increases the child's desire for sucking satisfaction, which is his means of coping with stress. In other words, if the weaning process itself produces stress, the desire for sucking gratification increases as an important means for minimizing stress. A vicious circle is set in motion. Avoid it by weaning your baby after he has had considerable experience with the cup.

How long will weaning take?

Longer than most people think. The most successful techniques allow the child who can feed himself to continue to have one bottle at some time during the day, which usually turns out to be bedtime. Generally speaking, it is much easier for your child to give up the bottle during the day than to give it up when he needs to suck to relax and go off to sleep. The reason is that going off to sleep involves a need to regress to earlier stages of development in order to detach oneself from the objects of the waking life. Eventually when you stop the bottle even at bedtime, your child may want you to spend some time holding, rocking, and cuddling him or perhaps reading him an additional story or two. Do this, because your child needs your help outgrowing his need to suck to relax.

Incidentally, we all know that many adults find a "night-cap" (which is an alcoholic stimulant) or a warm glass of milk necessary in order to relax and sleep. Other adults engage in primitive fantasies which are sexual and arouse the need for some kind of self-stimulation or masturbation. The phenomenon involved seems to be that a person going off to sleep experiences a diminution of inhibitions, which in some way facilitates regressive behavior and the need for infantile satisfactions. I know one thirty-four-year-old woman executive, quite successful and without neurotic symptoms, who confesses that she still sucks her thumb as she goes off to sleep.

What will happen if I wean my
baby too soon?

Weaning your baby too soon will tend to prolong his desire for sucking and encourage other means of oral grati-fication. A child weaned too soon is frustrated during an early stage in his life, the oral stage, when he has little tolerance for frustration. He may start to distrust the people who have caused his distress. He may find it increasingly difficult to relax and may withdraw from reality by sleeping, which at least removes the frustration he experiences when awake.

Severely frustrating your baby's sucking needs can predis-pose your child to serious emotional problems. He will have a very low frustration tolerance and a need for immediate gratification, particularly gratification achieved without effort by the recipient. An ability to put off immediate gratification for later, greater satisfaction can be a manifestation of improper weaning.

Are there problems if I wait too
long to wean my child?
Weaning your child too late is by no means as detrimental as doing it too soon. What usually happens is that the child's mother puts off weaning because she enjoys her child's dependency. If the mother is inclined to encourage that dependency, rewards her child for his dependency, and does not wean him, her child will be less apt to develop more mature characteristics. He may grow up to expect to be gratified without exerting himself. He may not learn to appreciate the rewards of initiating activity. Some theorists speculate that in a culture which allows the direct expression of a passive, dependent relationship between child and mother, so the weaning is delayed, alcoholism is minimal because the child doesn't later need to find indirect means of gratifying his oral needs. Statistics show, for example, that Jewish people, who supposedly prolong maternal dependency and offer plenty to eat during childhood, have a low incidence of alcoholism.

Are there any problems in
switching from breast-feeding
to bottle-feeding?
Some mothers who choose to breast-feed their babies decide after a short period of time, perhaps a month or two, to wean the child from the breast to a bottle. Your baby may balk a bit at first, but he will adapt. Some people speculate that an infant may interpret your switching him to a bottle as rejecting him. I doubt that your baby has the capacity to interpret the transition so harshly. He reacts, if he does, simply because he is not familiar with the newer bottle.

My position is supported by the common observation that a baby will not take a feeding from one person yet happily takes his feeding from someone else. We know a baby reacts to the way he is held and moved about, and I am inclined to think that there are other factors that have not yet been explored experimentally. For example, I have often wondered whether the smell and perhaps even the taste of the person feeding a child influences the child's receptivity. Generally speaking, it is a good idea, even if you are breast-feeding your baby, to give him an occasional bottle so that a bottle feeding is not totally foreign. It may become necessary if you must travel away from home. Most babies adjust to this procedure and enjoy both the bottle and the breast. Incidentally, having a breast-fed baby appreciate an occasional bottle allows his father the pleasures of feeding an infant, an event which I think every father enjoys.

*If I am expecting a new baby,
should I wean my other child
beforehand?*

No. Generally this will create problems. If your child is still sucking on a bottle or a breast, attempts to wean him may be initially successful. Unfortunately, your older child will probably want the bottle again when you return from the hospital. After all, the new infant is getting the breast or the bottle together with an awful lot of attention. Your older child logically and understandably decides he wants the same, and he regresses to the breast or the bottle. As this pattern is very common, I feel you are wise to allow your older child to feed as he has been feeding. In a matter-of-fact way and when he is at an appropriate age, begin weaning him without associating it in any way with the new baby. It will be much easier for your older child to relinquish his bottle if he does not associate it with decreased parental attention and affection. Just for the record, some mothers breast-feed two children at once, though this is rare.

Nature has things organized in a most magnificent way.

Many people know that breast-feeding tends to have contraceptive effects and that a mother is less apt to become pregnant while breast-feeding a child. Throughout history, some mothers have breast-fed their babies for this reason. I am impressed by nature's system because breast-feeding would tend to space children in a family functionally. In effect, a baby would be weaned before siblings began to compete for attention. There may be another part of nature's plan. If a mother were to breast-feed her child until the child was properly weaned, she would be unlikely to have children less than two years apart, or more likely three. And this seems to me to be the most satisfactory interval. It minimizes stress on the mother and the difficulty siblings sometimes have when they are too close in age.

Chapter V

◑⟩◐⟨◑⟩◐⟨◑⟩◐⟨◑⟩◐⟨◑⟩◐⟨◑⟩◐

Toilet Training

*What does toilet training mean
to my child?*

Toilet training is your child's opportunity to master his body and control his behavior by developing a completely independent response to internal physical sensations of pressure. He learns to go voluntarily to a toilet to deposit his body's products. This mastery is very different from previous accomplishments, such as being weaned, because your child is developing the emotional capacity to withhold any action or perform it at will just at the time he is becoming physiologically able to control his sphincter muscles. Prior to this time, your child had little impulse control, expressing his feelings without delay. Now he can withhold an action and directly express his negativism.

We are all familiar with this stage in emotional growth. Children close to two years of age tend to be negativistic, more likely to reject your ideas than to accept them. You probably have noticed that you can frequently get your child to do what you want by asking him to do the opposite. Saying "Don't put that shirt on" leads to an unending harassment until you give in. Your child is not being mean or rebellious when he reacts this way; he is simply discovering that he can withhold those things you want from him. He is showing his assertiveness and his decreasing dependence on you. His behavior frustrates you, but it does reflect your child's growing independence. What all this means for toilet training is that you can make your child go into the bathroom, but you can't make him go. And he knows it. It is not coincidence that toilet activities and toilet training in particular are the primary tasks at this stage of your child's development.

Can I help my child with toilet training?

Yes, you can, provided you help properly. Your child does require assistance in learning to master his body and control his impulses to defecate and urinate. You should realize first of all that you are limited to helping your child master the task by himself. Your goal is his independent capacity to control his toilet functions. The process is the goal, not the bodily products. All too often parents devote their attention to the product, and the product itself brings forth admiration, excitement, and love, and its absence produces rejection, hostility, and annoyance.

Generally speaking, your child will adopt your attitude toward being trained, and basically I know of no parent who is not delighted when his child gives up diapers. This means your child will, if he is physiologically capable, try to conform to your desires if you have enough patience to give him the chance and if you don't allow your own preconceptions to interfere. All too often parents approach toilet training with advice which, passed on from generation to generation, has become cultural prejudice. What they lack is any understanding of what toilet training means to the child himself.

Some parents see toilet training as associated with their child's intellectual capacity. It is not. Middle-class parents for many generations have used training as a means of comparing children's abilities and pride themselves on early training. This is senseless. All you should do—and this is hard enough—is approach training with an understanding attitude, displaying endless patience, waiting for your child to be physiologically ready, and continually promoting your child's independent ability to control toilet functions.

How should I toilet-train my child?

Your child should be toilet-trained by an interested and concerned parent. An attitude of indifference on your part will communicate to your child that you don't have any real concern about training, which is usually not the case. You will be encouraged in your task by remembering that children generally try to fulfill their parents' expectations. Strangely, these expectations can best be realized if your child has a sense of self-satisfaction and a sense of his own achievement rather than a sense of fulfilling your wishes. Although you should explain your interest in a child's toilet training, the intensity of your concern should not be so great as to be interpreted by your child as the equivalent of love or loss of love. If you place too much emphasis on successful toilet behavior, your child may get the idea that he can please you by defecating in the acceptable way or make you angry by not doing it that way. If you inadvertently communicate that the way your child defecates or urinates is very important to you, your child then has the capacity to control your feelings. And when your child is in control of you, you have violated a cardinal rule.

What you must do is not allow your own feelings to be markedly influenced by whether your child defecates or urinates or not. Restrain yourself to showing concern for helping him accomplish his particular task, that is, normal toilet behavior, using his own resources. Begin to let your child know that going to the toilet is expected of him. Adopt a patient, matter-of-fact attitude about your expectations. Let me say again that toilet training requires great patience, since your child will be sporadic in his successes. Mistakes will occur, and regressive behavior will take place from time to time. Help him through those times when he has accidents. Even successful toilet training is accompanied by occasional mistakes.

How long will it take me to train my child?

That's not really important. Anyway, it depends on when you start to train your child. If you begin the toilet training process when the child is very young, it will take you longer than if you begin when your child is about two. In general, toilet training usually takes somewhere between one month and one year.

It is unrealistic to expect your child to be completely toilet-trained within two or three weeks without an occasional accident. Often your child who seems to be trained will regress or want to go back to diapers if there is some stress in his life such as the birth of a sibling, a parental conflict, or some other traumatic event. This type of regression often happens after treatment in a hospital or after you have gone away on a vacation. Even if you go away for as little as one night, you may return to find that your child shows his rebelliousness by beginning to soil.

Some children will show the opposite behavior; that is, rather than soil, they tend to hold back and are unwilling to go to the toilet. They can become severely constipated. Incidentally, prolonged constipation, going beyond a week or so, not only represents a physical hazard but indicates some psychological problem, usually relating to a child's feeling of anger toward his parents.

*What happens if I start training
very early?*

If you begin toilet training your child very early, which means when he is under the age of fifteen months but more particularly under a year, you may create problems in the personality development of your child. Young children don't have the capacity to understand what toilet training is all about. Nor do they have enough voluntary control over their bodies to exert muscular control on a consistent basis. Because their muscular control is not quite adequate, they are extremely prone to accidents, which may make them feel like failures since they cannot always comply with your expectations. They fear you will withhold love and affection for their failure. It is not good for your child to feel you may be angry, because all children of this age see parental anger as equivalent to abandonment.

If you stress toilet training early in your child's life, he begins to feel that neatness, cleanliness, orderliness, and control lead to positive parental responses. After all, you do seem pleased and enthusiastic when he does a certain thing in a certain place in a certain amount at a certain time in a certain way. A connection develops in your child's mind between a particular ritual of neatness and cleanliness and parental acceptance and love. Alternatively, he suspects that if he does not produce this same amount in the same way at the same time according to your expectations, he may face rejection and abandonment. A very young child fears this to the point of panic.

There is another problem with training a very young child. His bowels move, and lo and behold, a certain result takes place. The very young child is unable to see any connection between his own acts and the whole sequence that takes place. Depositing his feces in the toilet produces a certain happy parental response, even though he did not control the act. Accordingly, your child might develop a belief that things just happen without his having anything to do with them. In fact, he did not have anything to do with the act, the flow of his feces. This action happened spontaneously, and his parents reacted to something he had no control over. This sequence of events, repeated several times, can give your child a feeling that certain events take place magically or are in some way externally controlled.

Then, too, if you train a child very early, your child may feel that you, not he, are controlling his body. He may purposely allow all his bodily functions to be controlled by you. If that happens, you are improperly accepting the responsibility of controlling your child's body. In extreme cases mothers have been known to give their children enemas weekly, biweekly, or in some other predetermined manner. They are quite literally taking control of the child's internal functions and forcing him against his will to produce some object whose appearance provides the child's parents with much apparent gratification. Needless to say, when any child experiences this ritual over and over again, he may either rebel or panic at the fact that someone else is controlling his internal functions. Sometimes a child unhappily learns to accept and take pleasure in this kind of stimulation. This latter adaptation contributes to a personality that relies upon someone else to stimulate anal functions. The individual may even enjoy the sensation.

But aren't some children trained
before they are one year old?

Many parents have established what appears to be toilet training before a child's first birthday. I am skeptical. In getting a detailed description of what was accomplished, I usually find that the child was not actually toilet-trained, but that his parents had discovered a certain time when the child was inclined to have a bowel movement. Each day at the appointed moment, they simply picked up the child, ran to the toilet, and placed him on it just in time. This is not real toilet training, since toilet training implies that your child controls himself voluntarily.

If your child is merely conditioned to urinate or defecate upon a certain signal, such as being placed on a potty seat, he does not really have independent control. To your child, it is almost as if some external force controlled his bodily functions. As we have seen, this gives your child a somewhat distorted view of cause-and-effect relations. He will not understand that it is he, at his own direction, who is causing his bowels to move when he pleases, namely, when he is on the toilet.

While this distinction may not seem to be very important physiologically, from a psychological viewpoint it is absolutely a key one. Your child's sense of self-esteem and his feelings of well-being are based upon his capacity to express and control his own impulses. He must learn that acceptable toilet training depends on himself, not upon someone else or upon a magical sequence of events.

*When is the proper time to
toilet-train my child?*

Generally speaking, your child's nervous system must be mature enough so that the sphincter muscles which are involved in holding back the spontaneous passage of feces are sufficiently developed for your child to be capable of exerting control. Any capacity for effective control usually is not developed until your child is twelve months of age, and full control of these muscles usually does not occur until some time past eighteen months of age. For this reason, toilet training is often not accomplished until your child is past eighteen months and usually not until he is somewhere between two and three years of age.

I have found it advisable to wait to toilet-train your child until he can talk, since he will need verbal communications to tell you that he has an internal pressure and needs relief. This communication lets you know that your child is in distress and needs assistance in going to the toilet. Perhaps it is not entirely coincidence that when your child is capable of connecting a spoken word or a signal with his internal feelings, he is generally ready for toilet training.

It also helps to know that between eighteen months and two years of age children copy behavior and seem to get a sense of satisfaction out of imitating grown-ups. You will find the training process much easier if you wait at least until your child shows a tendency to want to imitate.

When your friends start training their child before you do, remember this: studies have shown that the age at which a child becomes toilet-trained is in no way related to the age when his parents begin toilet training. Middle-class parents are inclined to begin toilet training earlier, whereas lower-class parents often start later. There is no difference in the age at which their children ultimately achieve toilet training.

Will it help my child to have a
demonstration of proper toilet
behavior?

Yes. While it is not necessary for a father to train his son, a little boy should at least have seen a male use the bathroom. By the same token, a little girl should also have the experience of seeing her mother. Incidentally, children often express considerable curiosity about the way the opposite sex engages in toilet functions. Little girls are notorious for wanting to stand up when they urinate and make all kinds of attempts to do so. Unfortunately, this practice is very disappointing for a little girl and can even be humiliating. Equally notoriously, boys have a sense of pride in being able to urinate standing up. They often express their supposed strength by seeing how far they can urinate. This common behavior leads some theorists to speculate about feelings of envy that females may have for men. Some of these same theorists speculate that being able to urinate for some distance in front of one's self unconsciously reflects the capacity of the individual to project himself forward. They say it reflects the individual's desire to project himself ahead in time. Of course little boys invariably match themselves up against each other to see who, according to this theory, can project himself farthest into the future.

I am not sure I accept these notions, although they have a certain amusing quality. I don't really believe that little girls try to urinate standing up in an attempt to be like boys or necessarily as an expression of envy. I believe they do it simply because children explore all kinds of things and try doing things in all kinds of ways. At every stage of development, children are inclined to play other roles. Boys trying to emulate girls and girls trying to emulate boys show natural tendencies that reflect a child's natural curiosity. Obviously, if these exploratory desires dominate behavior or continue over long periods of time, your child may have some emotional problem.

Is it harder for me to train a son, or a daughter?

The literature on child development indicates that girls seem to toilet-train earlier than boys. I am not sure that this is in fact so, but at the same time I am not able to say that it isn't. I am inclined to think that since mothers are the ones who do most of the toilet training, it would be easier for them to train a girl than a boy, particularly since children imitate behavior. This being the case, girls would indeed achieve success faster than boys.

Why do some children wet only at night?

Training your child, if it is truly accomplished by helping him achieve control through his own means, usually results in control that survives through the night. In my experience, children who have been toilet-trained very early, or more accurately, conditioned rather than trained, demonstrate early bowel control but may wet for a much longer period of time. These children often wet their beds at night. Thus, if you toilet-train later rather than earlier, your child will more likely achieve bladder control at the same time he achieves bowel control.

There may be another factor. Many parents allow a child to have a diaper during the night even after the child is initially trained. They are anxious to avoid the inconvenience of changing sheets, should the child make a mistake. Do not fall into this unwise pattern. Allowing your child to have a diaper during the night can give him the impression that he may wet or soil at night even though it is not permissible to do so during the day.

You should realize that most of the time loss of bladder control occurs only occasionally and is related to emotional tensions. Sometimes wetting is the result of some constitutional or hereditary inability to wake up when the bladder has reached a certain level of tension. Thus, one finds in many families that bed-wetting occurs well into childhood and then seems to subside spontaneously. Sometimes pediatricians employ medication to help a child with this problem.

Should I use devices that ring
bells to wake a child?

I am unalterably opposed to these devices. They are supposed to work by ringing a bell when a child is wet, which is supposed to condition the child to a certain bladder pressure, which is supposed to be the signal to wake up and go to the toilet. In short, the manufacturers hope that waking the child up when his bladder reaches a certain pressure will train him to do so without the ringing bell. Although these devices sometimes do work, I feel it is more important for your child to learn to use his own resources to achieve control. Relying upon any external device to do the job robs your child of his opportunity.

I am also wary of automatic conditioning devices, because I have seen too many instances where they have affected the child's personality. I have seen cases where male youngsters trained this way become sexually impotent later in life. I think they have become unconsciously accustomed to an external cue, passively offered, to start some internal mechanism of bodily control. These men always expected some external signal to set off a physiologic response. They do not expect to have to exert any effort. Since the same external apparatus is involved in sex as in bladder relief, it is understandable how conditioning urinary functions to a bell can in some way establish a need for some external cue to initiate sex activity. But in spite of my curiosity over the cause of the sexual problem in such men, and the clinical evidence I have just described, I have never prescribed a bell to cure impotence.

Should I let my child touch his
feces if he seems to want to?

Yes, but under controlled conditions. It is quite common for your child, who is curious about everything at the age of two or three, to want to touch his feces, since they are his "own product." After all, he does not know that feces are bad, ugly, or disgusting, and he wants to explore. Allow your child to touch his feces, maybe in the bathtub, and at the same time inspect them. Satisfy your child's curiosity, but do not make a beneficial exploration experience into a creative enterprise. Once your child has satisfied his curiosity, his inquisitiveness will end.

Generally speaking, you should avoid associating the products of toilet functions with feelings of disgust or distaste. A matter-of-fact attitude is better. If you take a prohibitive attitude, you may increase your child's fascination and his desire to play with his feces. On the other hand, if you offer encouragement, your child may comply with your wishes. He will generally place greater emphasis on his feces than necessary. There was a time when child-care experts encouraged parents to allow their children free play with their feces to avoid interfering with developing creativity. I am glad that that day has passed.

Incidentally, you can make too much of body products in another way, which unfortunately happens too often. Some enlightened or "psychologically oriented" parent, attempting to make his child feel secure, expresses great joy when his child succeeds in defecating in the toilet. Following this feat, the parent overreacts by calling everyone in the family to come to see what has been done, gives the child a big hug and kiss, and then promptly flushes the toilet. Finding a perplexed child standing there staring is quite understandable. After all, his parents have just made a great fuss over, and placed great value on, his feces, only to flush them away. If you are inclined to make a big fuss and bother, it would be more appropriate to give your child the chance to flush the toilet himself. Children very often have a sense of pride in their accomplishment and want to show off their product. They may even want to wave bye-bye as the feces pass down the toilet bowl.

*What does it mean if my child
regresses after he has been
trained?*

You should expect periodic regression in the course of toilet training. Remember, until now your child has been defecating and urinating at will. Suddenly he is being urged to control himself. It is not easy for anyone to give up a freedom he has been used to. If your child regresses after he is trained, it may be a chance happening or it may occur when your child is nervous, tense, or under pressure. Perhaps the most frequent cause is the birth of a sibling shortly after a child has been toilet-trained. Many parents attempt to toilet-train a child early if they are expecting another child. Quite understandably they want to avoid the difficulties of caring for two children in diapers at the same time. Unfortunately, pushing toilet training when a new child is anticipated more often than not causes regression when the sibling is born. No upstanding, self-respecting child could tolerate giving up diapers when the new intruder is given all kinds of love, affection, and attention while being attended to and diapered.

Chapter VI

❀❁❀❁❀❁❀❁❀❁❀❁❀

Discipline and Punishment

Should I discipline my child?

Yes. Discipline is absolutely necessary for a child. Discipline is essential to healthy growth and development and is an integral part of learning. Rules, regulations, laws, and principles govern almost all intellectual activity, be it in science or in the arts and humanities. When we speak of discipline in childhood, we are concerned with a similar process. I don't mean to stray, but I do want to emphasize the meaning of discipline in its broadest sense to separate it from punishment—a term that many people have come to use interchangeably with discipline.

The rules, regulations, and expectations that regulate your child's conduct constitute discipline. Teaching your child to follow the rules and regulations helps him adjust to the world and engage in socially acceptable behavior. In this way your child learns to be aware of the rights of others and to respect these rights. Moreover, discipline helps direct your child's interests outside himself so that he does not function solely in terms of his own impulses without regard for other people's feelings.

Discipline serves many other functions for the growing child. It establishes that the world is an organized place and that consistently organized limitations make things predictable. Discipline provides structure and contributes to an understandable consistency. Language, for example, is a form of organization that has rules and regulations and contributes to understanding among people. We often speak of a particular field of study such as physics or chemistry as a "discipline," since that field has within it a set of principles, concepts, and laws that facilitate communication between scholars in a meaningful way. Without discipline there is no communication, only chaos.

Let me stress the fact that discipline is *not* synonymous with punishment. These two terms are frequently confused when describing the way parents deal with children. While punishment is basically different from discipline, its existence is implied in the concept of discipline. Punishment is a sort of "fine," or price you pay, for deviating from the established rules and regulations.

Disciplining your child tells him that you are concerned about his behavior and care how he acts. Establishing discipline for your child and enforcing it can be considered one expression of love. The average child will interpret a lack of discipline as meaning you don't care. But the prerequisite for effectively disciplining your child is for the child to know that you care about him.

*When is my child ready to be
disciplined?*

Your child is ready to be disciplined when he begins to crawl and walk and move around in his environment. He will be starting to control his own movements, picking things up if he wants to or putting them down if he wants to. While your child's physical readiness is an important prerequisite for instituting discipline, perhaps the most vital necessity is that your child has experienced a sincere and deep sense of love and security from the significant adults in his life whom he has learned to trust.

As I have pointed out, discipline is not only ineffective during early infancy but it can prevent your young child's developing a sense of trust in others. If your child has not developed a sense of trust in his parents, it will be difficult, if not impossible, for you to discipline him. Discipline requires that a child has experienced a feeling of love, and it is the warmth of this feeling that motivates your child to follow through on the rules and regulations you institute. After all, if your child has never known the love of his parents, there is little for him to fear losing if he does not try to meet your expectations.

Am I the best person to discipline my child?

The best people to discipline any child are those in whom he has a sense of trust, those who have offered him protection and have satisfied his needs. The adults who love a child are by far the most effective people to discipline him. Since parents are generally the people for whom the child has these feelings most strongly, they are generally the ones who ought to be the most effective disciplinarians.

I don't mean to debase human beings by referring to canines, but most people readily acknowledge that the best person to train a dog is the one the dog trusts most, the one who feeds the dog and takes care of it. The dog obeys that person in order to maintain the warmth of the relationship and to ensure that pleasures stemming from the relationship will continue. In the same way, when the child knows his parents love him, he has a strong inclination to follow the disciplinary rules in order to preserve that love. But in order for the child to fear even a temporary loss of parental love, the child must know what love is.

Then my close relationship with
my child makes me an effective
disciplinarian?

Yes. Because you are capable of withholding the love and affection which your child wants, in response to any unacceptable behavior. To set limits and teach rules and regulations, that is, to discipline, it is essential that you have both a reward and a deprivation structure in order to help your child *feel* as well as recognize the relationship between the way he behaves and the rules he must follow. The most effective reward-deprivation structure is based on a parent's reactions to his child's actions. When your child behaves properly, you can and should show a sense of pride and pleasure in reaction to what he does. If he does not behave as you expect, you can show dissatisfaction and annoyance. Believe me, if your child was happy as an infant, had his needs satisfied, and established trust in people, particularly in you, he is aware of your negative reaction, your annoyance, which will appear to him as a temporary loss of parental love. You must recognize the power of your position as a parent when you are in a position to set up a reward-deprivation structure based on *your* reactions. This configuration motivates your child toward behavior that is acceptable to you.

Incidentally, your close relationship with your child will help in another way. Young children are notorious for emulating the behavior of other people. Most parents are aware of this factor and behave accordingly. For example, they are usually careful about using "bad language" because their children will be inclined to pick it up. If you never say "thank you" or "excuse me," your child will copy you. Children are most likely to emulate the people they trust most, those who are the greatest source of affection, love, and security. That should be you. If, when your child copies the patterns of life of which you approve, you show approval and increased affection, he will continue this behavior. He is, in effect, incorporating them into his own repertoire of responses. By so doing he is developing socialized patterns of behavior that are by definition acceptable to others, in this case to you. Not only that, your child is adopting a rule of regulation you are teaching him and internalizing it.

*I take it you feel internalizing
discipline is good?*

Absolutely. It helps your child establish a sense of "right and wrong" and in so doing contributes to civilized behavior. Eventually, a child's sense of right and wrong becomes what we call a "conscience." A conscience is in effect a code of ethics that exists within a person, and when this code is violated the person has feelings of guilt. Potential feelings of guilt are crucially important to impulse control. Guilt is a most unpleasant feeling, and its unpleasantness serves to motivate people to avoid doing those things that are unacceptable to their consciences. If a child grows up without developing an effective conscience, if he lacks an internalized set of values, he is inclined to follow his impulses regardless of what damages others may suffer. Usually, the only worry a "conscienceless" person has is the possibility of being caught and punished. He has no concept of right and wrong. Often his behavior is unacceptable to both individuals and society generally.

*Can you give me an example of
the disciplinarian in action?*

Certainly. The example I've selected involves a young child a little less than a year old, but the principle described applies all through childhood. Your young baby beginning to crawl around finds an electric outlet. He shows a normal, natural curiosity and begins to poke his fingers in the holes. You probably will react by raising your voice and saying

"No, no" emphatically, with an annoyed expression on your face to communicate to your child that his behavior is not acceptable. Your own reaction is not only appropriate, it may save your child's life. When you communicate your feelings and show some reaction, your child learns what he can do and what he can not. But let me continue with this illustration to point out that your first reaction is only the beginning, not, as too many parents believe, the end.

The likelihood is that your child will try poking his fingers into the outlet again to see if you will have the same reaction. Of course, you should. After having tried poking his fingers into the openings two or three times in succession, your child may try his other hand, looking carefully to see if you still disapprove. Believe it or not, your child is behaving like a well-disciplined scientist who is testing a series of hypotheses to find out what is causing your reaction. To continue the test, the child may crawl quickly to another light plug on the other side of the room and begin all over again. If you are still present while this additional experiment is taking place, and if each time your child gets the same reaction, whether he's testing the light plug on one side of the room or the other, or whether he's using the fingers of the left hand, the right hand, or possibly the elbow, or perhaps even an object, your child will eventually realize that he must not poke anything into any electric outlet.

Unfortunately, a busy parent often does not take the time to supervise a child's experiments until the youngster reaches the proper conclusion. In this case, suppose you left the room following the first poking episode. If so, your child will likely have learned *not* that it is unacceptable to poke his fingers into the light fixture, but that it is unacceptable to poke his fingers into it while you are in the room. Thus, when a lesson like this is being taught, you should stay with your child long enough to make sure that he has tested all the possibilities and clearly understands what your feelings and reactions are. In short, you should remain with him until you have taught your child what you want him to know. Take sufficient time to give your child a chance to test out *all* the possible combinations and permutations to establish what is acceptable and what is not. In my experience, a child who has conducted a series of experiments like these usually ends with a big smile and a great sense of satisfaction in having solved the mystery. He now understands what it is that caused his parent's negative reaction.

A child is fascinated by this kind of learning and, indeed, tests his conclusions periodically to see if he gets the same reaction from his parent. He really is not trying to make your life miserable, even though it may seem so at the moment. He is simply enjoying the fact that he is able to elicit specific reactions from others through his own behavior. When a child has become aware that his behavior has stimulus value for others, he will be much more inclined to use it to elicit *positive* reactions in others, rather than negative reactions. The reason is that any child, by gaining positive reactions, reestablishes his feeling of being loved because people react to positive behavior in a positive way. There is no question that any child enjoys rewards for positive behavior.

Must I always discipline my child?

Yes. In essence, discipline is the consistent application of the rules and regulations you have established. If you are erratic or inconsistent in setting standards for acceptable behavior and if you fail to enforce them unfailingly, your child will sense that your rules are weak. After all, if you climb a tree, you quickly learn to hold on and not lose your footing. You learn this, because if you don't, you fall down (never up) and it hurts (it never feels good).

You might like to think of discipline as rules of behavior that are like the rules of a game. Consistency in enforcing the rules is very important to maintain "the game," as any child who changes the rules of the game to suit himself finds out—when the game stops because no one else will play. In fact, children enjoy playing games that have rules, a very strong indication that children not only like rules, but seek them out. Children's attitudes toward each other are often the result of their capacities to follow through on "the rules of the game."

Establishing rules and regulations has another function. They establish a certain predictability between a child's action and the world's reaction. Predictability decreases anxiety and uncertainty, since we are often anxious simply because we are uncertain and unable to make any prediction with any degree of certainty.

What happens if I am not consistent?

If you are not consistent in your expectations about your child's behavior, he becomes anxious. Often this anxiety shows up in a great deal of activity and sometimes in hyperactivity. You are unpredictable. He feels vulnerable and unprotected. Many, many times I have treated children who feel that their parents don't care about them. Careful examination of their behavior reveals their attempts to get their parents to show any kind of feeling toward them, even rage. These children may even feel that their parents don't care enough about them to be angry with them.

When you are inconsistent, much of your child's behavior will be misbehavior, since he will test you to see how far you will go. You may feel that he is "driving you up the walls," but his intent is not to make you uncomfortable. Your child is simply searching for the rules in order to test them sufficiently to be sure that he will be protected by them. He can relax only when he feels that you are strong enough and concerned enough to show him, through your consistency, that you care.

Problems stemming from inconsistent discipline are sometimes created not because parents are inconsistent in their handling of a child but because they allow other people to set rules and regulations upon occasion. This inconsistency occurs when a baby nurse enforces rules and regulations or when a child is cared for by grandparents or when you listen to other people telling you how to take care of your children.

Reasonable rules and regulations promote discipline. If the disciplinary rules you set are so unrealistic that you cannot enforce them consistently without feeling cruel, you will surely be inconsistent. It is not uncommon and is often understandable that when you are harassed by your child, you set extremely rigid rules such as "If you don't finish your lunch, you must spend the whole afternoon in your room." You will find it extremely difficult to enforce this without feeling you are putting your child in solitary confinement. But reneging makes you an inconsistent disciplinarian. You have put yourself in a position of being either cruel or inconsistent. For this reason, the regulations you set must be reasonable, protective, and enforceable.

Don't these regulations interfere with my child's sense of freedom?

No. On the contrary, your child can have no sense of freedom unless there are some restrictions. Unfortunately, some adults believe the absence of regulations and rules facilitates a sense of freedom. They insist on creating an atmosphere of "permissiveness," a word with positive and pleasant connotations. All too often it is employed to describe a total absence of rules. In my way of thinking, if you set up a permissive situation and refuse to establish discipline, your child invariably interprets your action as indifference. When he feels you are indifferent, he assumes you don't care. This is disastrous.

Even worse, a child who is brought up "permissively" often

lacks adequate internal controls and destroys things right and left. Such a child becomes a "monster." While he may not be basically destructive by nature, no one, particularly not his parents, has made any attempt to set limits on his behavior that would help him channel his energy into useful or constructive activities. Incidentally, all psychologists and psychiatrists know that many procedures that are inherently constructive are developed by channeling potentially destructive impulses. For example, every scientific discovery implies a certain element of destructiveness insofar as the new discovery destroys preexisting ideas. Scientists, in effect, are constantly trying to knock down ideas, but they are also attempting to replace them with something better. Only by regulating behavior is it possible to channel destructive impulses into useful activity.

Many children reared in an atmosphere of "permissiveness" become terribly inhibited. They are simply terrified by their own destructive impulses. Since there are no adults around who will set limits for them to help them control their impulses, they will refrain from all activity. These children become terribly constricted. If you ask them are they having fun, they tell you they will have to think about it.

I have seen many adults with behavior problems who came out of such an environment. They find it extremely difficult to make decisions, they have difficulty projecting themselves into the future, and very often they find it impossible to savor any pleasure. The limits their own parents did not set they set themselves, and more often than not, these limits are more restrictive than those their parents would have set. Spontaneity is utterly lacking.

*Does this mean that punishment
is advisable?*

Punishment is a necessary evil at times. If your feelings and reactions are not sufficient to elicit acceptable behavior or suppress unacceptable behavior, it may be necessary to administer a punishment. But don't confuse this with discipline. Discipline represents the rules, regulations, and controls that limit acceptable behavior. Punishment is a price the child pays for disobeying the rules. Punishment and discipline are not interchangeable.

If you threaten punishment, be prepared to follow through. Some parents constantly threaten a child with punishments only to back down. This is inadvisable. You are being weak, and you are undermining the rules and regulations the punishment is supposed to support. You should not make any threat unless you are fully prepared to carry it out. You are better off on occasion ignoring your child's misdeed, instead of threatening a punishment that you don't administer. And if you can't think of a fair punishment, don't threaten any. Of course, if you expect to be a good parent, you'd better not let this happen too often.

How do I establish standards of
punishment?

As far as possible, the punishment should fit the "crime." Depriving a child of playing in a very important baseball game that he has greatly anticipated because he didn't brush his teeth in the morning is absolutely incongruous. Playing baseball has nothing to do with brushing one's teeth, and not brushing one's teeth is hardly a failure meriting punishment as severe as losing out on an important event to which your child has looked forward for a long time. It would be more appropriate to take him to the bathroom and watch him brush his teeth. The punishment should be both qualitatively and quantitatively equivalent to the child's misdeed.

When the intensity of a punishment is very great, your child may not learn what you are trying to teach. You may be trying to emphasize the importance of acting in a certain way. But your child sees your punishment as cruel and loses sight of his crime. He feels justified in thinking you are mean. He is utterly unable to consider his behavior as misbehavior, particularly when his suffering overshadows the main point. Milder forms of punishment are much more likely to convey a sense of wrongdoing to your child and will be more apt to modify his subsequent behavior in a constructive manner. Studies have shown over and over again that severe punishment simply makes a child feel that he has to avoid getting caught the next time.

Recently I encountered a child who, because he pushed a girl in class, was made to write "I will not push a girl" five hundred times. In discussion with him it became obvious that this punishment would not alter his behavior toward girls, but would alter his behavior toward his teacher. He was clear that the next time he would make sure the teacher wasn't looking. The ethical aspects of pushing girls didn't even enter his mind. He felt that he was justified and his teacher was unjustified.

If your child consistently misbehaves in one area, consider pointing this out to him and saying that you feel that a punishment must be established. Tell him that the punishment in all fairness should be decided upon by both of you, and ask what he considers fair. You will be amazed to find that his recommendation will quite likely be far harsher than anything you could have imagined. When I have employed this technique myself, I have been shocked to hear recommendations such as "Don't feed me for three weeks," or "Don't let me see any friends for a year." If you bring your child into the situation in this way, you are in a good position to monitor the punishment so that you can decrease its severity. You remain the "enforcing agency," but you show you have a sense of tenderness, protectiveness, and rational judgment.

To make a punishment effective in support of established discipline, you must control the situation. But at the same time you must show your concern for your child. You must take into consideration his feelings, and you must let him know you understand them. If you disregard your child's feelings, the punishment will not accomplish your purpose. For example, many parents have difficulty getting their children to keep their rooms in reasonable order. While one cannot expect a child to keep everything meticulously clean, a child does not have to take his clothes off and leave them all over the floor, never picking them up. Parents are exasperated by their inability to control this situation. If the parent announces that beginning the next day, he will from that point onward put into a box everything that he finds on the floor in the way of clothing that ought to be hung up or put in the laundry and that in order to get back his clothing the child must do fifteen minutes of work to assist his parent, the youngster will probably begin to feel more involved in the consequences of his behavior, and the parent will gain some control over the situation. A parent can take an apologetic attitude in enforcing this kind of punishment, explaining that all other efforts have failed and this procedure is the last alternative.

It is important to warn your child in advance when behavior can result in punishment. This warning gives him an alternative. He can either conform and avoid the punishment or misbehave and face the punishment. Which means that I think it is only fair to warn your child in advance if you are going to spank him, so that he at least has the choice of behaving or not behaving and knowing what the outcome will be. Incidentally, the spanking need not cause physical pain. The fact that you are showing your strength is sufficient, and a very mild spanking will be effective. Don't be surprised that young children feel compelled to cry when they have been spanked, even if the spanking didn't hurt.

When is punishment harmful?

When the punishment is disassociated from discipline, that is, when a punishment is disassociated from the rules and regulations you have established, then it is harmful. Punishment can also be harmful when there is no misdeed—in effect, when an innocent person is being punished. If the punishment exceeds the severity of the misbehavior and causes your child to see you as mean rather than protective, it does no good. Punishment can have detrimental effects when there is no time proximity between the misbehavior and the punishment itself. For example, a child who misbehaves on Monday morning and is told he will, therefore, not be allowed to do something he wanted to do on the following weekend may experience no feelings of remorse whatsoever at the time of his punishment. When the punishment is enforced, it is completely unrelated to anything that he *feels* has ever happened. He will be inclined to see the parents as mean and unjustified in punishing him. The punishment hurts, but it does not teach.

There are times when punishment offers some satisfaction to parents but has no relationship whatsoever to a child's behavior, perhaps when a parent has been angered by a child's behavior, loses control, and enforces an unwarranted punishment. When this happens, the child is confused, feels unprotected, and loses his sense of security in dealing with that adult. After all, if the grown-up who is supposed to offer protection loses control himself, the child is left feeling uncertainty about future events. This kind of punishment might best be considered as a case of adults being "mean."

Are you saying it's best to use
rewards rather than punishment
in the discipline of a child?

Yes. In general, it is better. Remember, however, that the rewards I recommend are your feelings and reactions to your child's behavior, and not some material reward. Providing a material reward for acceptable behavior tends to place greater emphasis on material things than one should, simply because, as nearly everyone knows, material satisfactions in life have never served to create any sustained sense of satisfaction. If you use material rewards in place of your approval, you deprive the child of recognizing the importance of human feelings and understanding the satisfactions of close relationships. At the same time, you create a connection between acceptable behavior and an object that represents acceptance and love. If you invariably reward your child with presents, he will develop a desire to acquire material things. Obviously, a child who has been taught to associate material objects with parental acceptance may demand more and more toys or more and more possessions simply because he feels unloved. No child is born acquisitive; he is taught to behave that way.

At the same time, if you deprive your child of his possessions in order to punish unacceptable behavior, you accentuate the value of his possessions and deemphasize the importance of the behavior in terms of its human meaning. Losing the object equals the loss of love. This means, in effect, that possession of the object is the equivalent of having love.

Often a child who has been constantly rewarded with objects or punished by having possessions removed uses this same technique in dealing with his parents and others. He learns to negotiate in material terms. He demands rewards for achievement and may show little motivation at school unless a parent promises to give some *thing* as a trophy for acceptable performance. Over and over I have been consulted by parents of young college students who lack motivation and refuse to study unless they are promised a new sports car if they achieve a *B* average. These children never seem to get any inherent pleasure out of what they do, since they tend to evaluate their accomplishments in terms of the material things that can be acquired by their efforts. A material, extracurricular reward undermines the basic pleasure that a child can gain from the learning process. Most children find learning rewarding simply because it satisfies their curiosity. It is the parent who confuses the picture by adding a material element.

Needless to say, this technique of reward has tremendous social implications because it introduces material acquisitions as a sign of success, achievement, and love. It lends itself to an attitude of materialism, greed, and acquisitiveness. It tends to place human values second to material values, and in so doing it allows people to ignore the effect their behavior has on the feelings of others. I have treated many adult patients who depended upon objects to gain a feeling of well-being. The objects represented a substitute for love. They constantly engage in looking for things, shopping around, and buying things. Many have reported to me that they feel unfulfilled unless each day they find some *thing* to add to their possessions. The patient's childhood history most often includes the use of objects as rewards for behavior.

Then you are basically recommending rewards that depend on my interest in, and affection for, my child?

Yes. Many parents pay no attention to a child unless he is doing something bad. These parents do not take the time to be involved with their child, nor do they show any interest in what a child is doing or in those activities that are currently meaningful to the child. The child of such parents is quick to learn that it is easier to get attention by bad behavior, and the resulting parental concern tends to reinforce this technique.

What these parents have forgotten is that using acceptance and affection as a reward sensitizes a child to the feelings of others. It can make a child more aware of the world. When you really get down to it, the marvel of parental love and its effectiveness in teaching life's important lessons is quite astounding. Using affection and acceptance teaches that rewards come from human interaction. Learning this will counteract the greed, hostility, and destructiveness that has plagued mankind. Nothing is more valuable and potentially gratifying to a parent than to relate to a child to teach him the value of human relationships. No matter how gratifying one's work and achievements may be, there can be no greater reward than bringing up a child who respects, loves, and is concerned with others in the world in which he lives.

Chapter VII

❂❖❂❖❂❖❂❖❂❖❂❖❂❖❂❖❂

Sex Education

Shall I tell my child the facts
about sex and reproduction?

Yes. If you don't, someone else will. There is no reason, logically, for withholding information about reproduction or sex from your child. Inquiring professionally among many parents about the sex education of their children, I have found that most parents believe in educating their children about reproduction and sex at an early age, in spite of the fact that many of these same people have not done it. Inquiring further into this paradox, I learned that many parents did not give their children information about reproduction simply because they did not know how to. Their reluctance was based more on their own anxiety and their own lack of knowledge than on the feeling that early knowledge about these normal life processes might have adverse effects. The typical reactions were: "I don't know how to go about it"; "I thought I'd wait and let someone else do it"; or "I didn't get around to doing it." Procrastination stemming from parents' feelings of inadequacy often left the child's questions unanswered.

A child should have the opportunity to learn about one of life's most fundamental experiences from his own parents, who are, after all, the most appropriate people to tell him the facts. Unfortunately, many parents' anxiety is not without cause, since they themselves are not as well informed as they should be. They do lack fundamental knowledge about how to discuss the subject with children. Many parents remember their own traumatic experiences and confused ideas, some of which stemmed from misinformation gathered from poorly informed people. Often parents remember being told about sex and reproduction by someone other than their parents, or not being told at all. Sometimes they recall finding out the facts after they had conjured up some outlandish notion about how the species reproduced itself. Offering erroneous information to placate your child and to delay having to deal with sex and reproduction directly doesn't go very far with the average intelligent child, since storks are hard to come by and no one has ever seen the counter in a department store where they sell babies. Isn't it strange how many of us have been poorly prepared by our own parents to cope with sex and reproduction? Yet we are inclined to perpetuate this error.

It is obviously important to be well informed about sex and reproduction for your own personal reasons, but it is absolutely crucial for educating your children. You must familiarize yourself with the facts and not rely simply on your own experiences. Many reputable books are extremely informative. Use them as a basis for the knowledge that you can interpret to your child at his level. Not telling your child the facts about reproduction is silly; transmitting misinformation is altogether foolish, if not actually damaging.

Is there a difference between describing the facts of reproduction and describing the feelings of sex?

Yes. And it is important to recognize the difference. When most young children ask their first questions, they are asking questions about reproduction, not about feelings of sex. Too often parents discuss sex when all the child actually wants to know about has to do with reproduction. Picture an anxious parent who has prepared himself in anticipation of his child's questions. When the moment arises, when the first question is asked, this eager parent may spew forth everything at once to get an unpleasant situation over with. He unloads on the child. This response will undoubtedly perplex the child, who may not be prepared to cope with all the information he is given. Some day it may be appropriate to tell your child about sex, that is, people's feelings of love and their physical attraction for each other, but at first this information is not essential. Most young children want concrete facts about physiology and who does what, where, when, and how. If your child is given good basic information regarding reproduction at the very beginning, and if future questions are brought to you, you will note an increasing concern with problems involving sexual feelings.

Does it harm my child to learn about the facts from someone other than me?

Yes. Information about reproduction and sex is very important information. You should be the one to tell your child so that he gets the idea that facts about sex and reproduction are not available just among strangers. If you avoid discussing sex or reproduction with your child, he can get the idea that these subjects are "forbidden," "dirty," or "unacceptable." You should take the responsibility for providing this information because it gives you an opportunity to learn what your child knows and to clear up any confused ideas he may have. And perhaps the most obvious reason for your being the primary source of your child's information lies in the fact that you can best control the kind of information he receives. The someone else who does it in all likelihood does not have the same sensitivity to your child as you do. You are more likely to get the message through to him properly.

While I am in favor of schools offering instruction about sex, I do recommend that you do not wait until your child goes to school before you tell him the facts. Most children begin asking questions long before they go to school. The school can amplify sexual knowledge and keep your child from feeling that discussing reproduction and sex is taboo. But it is not the school's responsibility to inform your child. It is your responsibility to provide the initial impetus and later to monitor information received from other sources, including school.

When do I tell my child?

You tell him when he begins to ask. Most children begin to ask questions at a very early age, two, three, four at the latest. Very often inquiries are precipitated by the advent of a new child or the dimensions of an "enlarged" mother. Your child's initial questions are usually quite direct and quite simple: "Where did I come from?" or "Where do babies come from?" When these first questions arise, answer them.

What do I tell him?

That depends upon his age when he asks, but in any case answer honestly, directly, and with information that he is capable of understanding. Don't deliver the full-scale lecture you have spent months preparing, and remember that your answers should preclude the possibility that your child will get the wrong information and proceed to generalize in a way that can lead to further confusion.

Let me give you an example. Some parents are inclined to explain that a "seed gets planted in the mommy's tummy," an explanation with two serious errors that can lead a child to great confusion. Number one, when you explain that "a seed gets planted," your child may picture someone taking a seed in his hand and planting it with a trowel. That is, after all, the kind of planting your child has experienced. One mother I know used this explanation; when her child asked "But how does the seed get planted?" she replied, "It gets planted in the mother but *not* with a rake." This explanation sufficed only until her child asked his next question, "But how *does* the seed get planted?" The second error in this explanation is the statement about where the seed is planted. The seed does not grow in the mother's "tummy," or even in the mother's stomach. The seed grows in the mother's uterus. For some strange reason, people are hesitant about using the word *uterus* and use *stomach* instead. The substitution can confuse your child and cause problems.

I have treated many young girls who complain of severe stomach aches and abdominal pains. On examination, I found they were anxious about maturing into women. Their pains were related to the idea that the stomach was the place where their child-bearing functions would take place. Along these lines, I have often observed children with confused ideas about impregnation, some with fantasies of conception taking place through the mouth. Some children may associate anal functions with child-bearing and may at the same time regard the anus as the place where the baby comes out of the mother. I would like to say flatly that there is no reason why your child cannot understand and learn that the uterus is *the* place in the body where the seed grows and that it is *near* the stomach. When I ask parents why they do not use this explanation, they say, "The child doesn't understand what the uterus is," hardly an intelligent reason for designating the stomach.

I have found, for the same reason, that many parents are afraid to use the words *vagina* and *penis* in describing the sex organs. Not only are these the appropriate words, but if you use this language from the beginning, there can be no confusion later. Most parents are afraid that their child would use the word *penis* in public to describe his "thing," which for some reason seems more permissible in some circles than the word *penis*. The irony is that everyone knows that the "thing" is a penis, and that "down there" refers to the vagina.

If you are a parent inclined to answer all of your child's questions directly, and if when he asks questions concerning sex matters your tone changes, the pacing of your words changes, and your whole mood changes, you will be telling your child that sexual information is special. I would prefer to have any child think of sexual information as similar to any other information, so that he adopts a somewhat matter-of-fact attitude, at least until he matures. Then, your child's general information takes on different meanings because he will have different feelings when he is capable of being aroused sexually.

Should my child's first exposure
to the facts of reproduction
involve humans?

Yes. Many parents feel that it is easier to begin by telling children about the "birds and the bees." Sometimes they take them to a farm or read them books about dogs and cats. They hope this approach will purify information about reproduction and decontaminate the facts from any sexual feeling.

Most youngsters couldn't care less about birds and bees. They are interested in the real thing: "Where did I come from?" Children feel suspicious when you sidestep a question or answer it in a roundabout way. Starting with the birds and the bees is simply a gimmick that parents use to get themselves "off the hook." We all know the boy who, having been told the "facts of life," adopted a facial expression denoting substantial fascination and went off to tell his friend "The birds and the bees do it, too."

How much should I tell my
child at one time?

Generally speaking, your answers should satisfy your child's curiosity honestly. The likelihood is that your child is asking these questions with the same natural innocence and curiosity that he may have about rockets getting to the moon. Once you answer his questions, he will ask further questions until his curiosity is satisfied.

I'm afraid I cannot tell you exactly how you should deal with your own child. But I suspect an average child can understand a presentation like this around the time he begins to ask simple questions:

A baby grows from a seed that is a little like the seed you plant in the garden. The seed grows in the mother's uterus, which is near her stomach. The mother has many seeds that can grow, but they come into the mother's uterus one by one about once each month. In order for the seed to grow, it is necessary for the seed to have some fluid from the father [or man] which grows inside the father and comes from his testicles. [This particular information is very fascinating to a boy, particularly if you explain where his testicles are and further explain that there is no fluid now and won't be any until around the time he becomes a grown-up.] The fluid [not to be confused with urine] that comes from the father is called *sperm*, which comes through his penis and gets into the uterus when he inserts his penis into the mother's vagina. When the sperm comes out of his penis into her vagina, it surrounds the mother's seed and starts it growing. Just as a plant seed will not grow until it is put in the ground, so the mother's seed will not grow without the father's sperm. When the seed does get fertilized, it begins to grow little by little and starts to take on all the details of a baby, little by little. When it is fully grown, the baby will be born.

It is extremely helpful if you have books or pictures available that show how a fetus grows in the uterus. Children are fascinated to see the different stages of pregnancy, and they will most likely ask questions about when the baby begins to move inside the mother, how it gets air and food, and how it knows when to get out, and how it comes out. All these questions should be answered in the same direct manner you used in your explanation. Your child should be told that the baby comes out after about nine months of growing inside the mother's uterus. The mother knows that it is ready to be born when she begins to feel tight muscle movements in her uterus. Your child can be told that when this begins to happen, the opening where the baby comes out, the vagina, begins to get larger so the baby can come out and that after the baby has been born, it begins to get smaller again. Incidentally, this is a perfect time to explain that the mother will go to the hospital where the doctor will help her have the baby.

If your child's questions have been prompted by your own pregnancy and these questions have been answered and his curiosity allayed, he will most likely regard your pregnancy with fascination and a certain kind of "academic interest." Most children, if they are informed, keep asking how big the baby is, and how long will it be before it comes out. They are greatly fascinated when they feel the fetal movements that begin to occur in the late months of pregnancy. Incidentally, discussing the events of pregnancy tends to buffer your child's apprehensions about having a new sibling, which suggests bringing him into the situation of the growing family at an early stage.

What about sexual feelings?

I have come to realize that many enlightened parents have been diligent and thorough in transmitting information about reproduction to their children. They have described the mechanics of sexual activity and reproduction in detail so that their children are informed. However, I find that in most cases, if not virtually all, they have neglected to prepare their children for dealing with sexual feelings. They have described the mechanical aspects of sexual activity, but they have never discussed the feelings of sexual arousal and various physical and emotional sensations that can be expected to occur. This information, incidentally, should *not* be included in answering a young child's questions, but should be included in sex education as your child begins to approach puberty, perhaps around the time of middle childhood when feelings of arousal occur, causing erections in boys and pleasurable clitoral sensations in girls.

I think you should tell adolescents and pre-adolescents that they may get special physical sensations if they touch members of the opposite sex, that they may have a desire to kiss them, and that kissing can result in all kinds of internal reactions ranging from a quickening heartbeat and rapid breathing to a moist vaginal sensation or an erection and possibly ejaculation. When your child understands that these reactions *normally* occur, he is less apt to feel embarrassed when they happen, because he will feel that what happened was normal, predictable, and even to be expected. If he has not been told about sexual feelings, a child may wonder if something is wrong with him. In this context, don't hesitate to discuss feelings of intense attachment for someone else, a "love" that makes you feel as if the other person is the only one who could satisfy you, the only person you will ever care to be close to. Explain that these attachments are natural feelings that often occur in conjunction with sexual arousal.

In discussing sex with a pre-adolescent or adolescent, don't make one of the most common mistakes. Many parents in moralizing about sex indicate that sex is beautiful *if* one is married. At the same time, they try to convey the attitude that sex relations are "bad" and possibly harmful before marriage. Base your position on premarital sex on moral, ethical, or religious grounds, not on some physiological change that is supposed to occur at the altar, since your child will find it extremely difficult to reconcile this apparent contradiction. After all, how can something be both beautiful and bad?

And that the contingency lies in a legal document? Too often the impression of badness prevails, and your child develops a feeling of guilt later on when engaging in sexual activity. Incidentally, parents sometimes inadvertently give the impression that sex is bad simply by referring to people who engage in sexual activity with a carefree attitude as being bad. A prohibitive attitude can also be conveyed by cautioning children to avoid contact with people who are less inhibited about sex.

If your child regards sexual feelings or sexual activity as bad or dirty, he may develop sexual desires that are satisfied only under circumstances that are forbidden or in conjunction with some fetish that is forbidden, bad, dirty, or unacceptable. I have treated many people who have been able to enjoy sexual activity only with someone who in their minds symbolizes lewdness or degradation. Often these people will debase a sexual partner to create the atmosphere they need for fulfillment. This behavior is intimately connected with an attitude that sex is dirty.

*Will my child remember all this
information when I am preparing him so far in advance?*

Yes. Even if at the time you talk to him the information seems very remote, maybe even meaningless, when the situation arises (as it surely will) which requires that he know about reproduction and sex, the facts will be readily available in your child's mind. Not only will he have the information he needs at the moment of crisis, he will remember that it was *you* who prepared him for the crisis. Accordingly, he will be more likely to turn to you with his other problems, which makes things easier for you. Incidentally, don't worry if your child does not react emotionally to what you say. That will happen later. For now, the important thing is that you explain in advance. Particularly remember, when you are discussing sex, to explain what feelings might occur, so that your child will not be overwhelmed by his emotional reactions.

What do I do if my child doesn't ask me about reproduction or sex?

As this rarely happens, try to figure out why your child does not ask. Usually someone else has been answering his questions. If you dealt with his questions in the past by avoiding them or giving him misinformation about the stork, your child may put off further questioning, since he senses you are not ready to give real answers to his questions. He may never question you again, simply because someone else came along and told him a lot more than you did. When this happens, some children will come back and tell you what someone told them. Then you're fortunate, because you do get an opportunity to amplify this information and clear up any misinformation that might have been included. Unfortunately, many children will regard having been given specific information by someone else as meaning that these facts are "forbidden knowledge," not to be discussed at all with their parents. They think it is wrong to know what they now know and will hide this information from their parents.

If my child knows about sex and doesn't discuss it with me, what should I do?

You should discuss it with him. Take the initiative and give him the chance to ask questions. Your child probably feels embarrassed and hesitant to ask you questions. After all, if he had questions, he probably would ask them, unless he was also embarrassed. By taking the initiative you will tell him that you don't mind his having the information. Attempt to convey to him that he can talk with you again, if he has any further questions. Remember that it is very hard to dissipate the embarrassment your child feels if he has learned the facts from someone else. Let me emphasize that you should avoid the temptation to be relieved that your child never asked and you never had to explain. Worse, you can be pleased that you child shows little interest in sex and never asked. I seriously doubt that this has ever been the reason a child never asked questions.

Then I should encourage my
child to discuss his questions
with me?

Absolutely. Your child should be encouraged to come to you with his questions. If you come across as a parent who is informative and who will help your child acquire the knowledge he needs, your child will come to you with his next questions. In fact, he will often check with you information he had gotten from other people, to get your opinion or ask you to confirm what he has heard. But the moment your child doubts the truth of what you tell him or learns that you "hedge," he will go elsewhere when he wants to know something. Incidentally, when I suggest that you encourage your child to talk to you I mean *encourage*, not force. If you try to force your child to ask you questions, you will create anxiety, which will interfere with any communication.

Is it wrong for my child to dis-
cuss sex with other children?

No. It's not. Anyway, there is nothing you can do about it. Think back in your own life, and you will remember when you talked about sex with your friends. Some children are proud to pass on to their peers what they know, because they gain a certain status by being so well informed. Some children for the same reason fabricate all kinds of ideas and pass them on.

When you answer your child's questions, it's not a bad idea

to mention that some other parents may not want their children to know all these same details and that it might be best for him not to discuss what he knows with other children. I realize this approach may undermine the feeling of openness and "matter-of-factness" I am emphasizing, but at the same time other parents may discourage their children from associating with your child who is so knowledgeable about what they consider "dirty things." You can point out to your child that not all children are told this information by their parents, because they feel that their children should not know until they are older, even though you feel it is perfectly all right for your children to know now. Taking this approach, rather than suggesting that your child not talk to his friends, may be better. You will have to make that choice yourself. Regardless of what you say, your child will pass on some facts to other children. Your caution will at least serve to warn your child that all children are not as well informed as he is.

Should I discuss my own sexual
experiences with my child?

No. I think you should say that sexual experiences are private, not subjects for public discusion. Refusing to discuss your sex life emphasizes this point. Children invariably wonder if their parents have intercourse, how often, and when. But children—and, I suspect, most adults—find it extremely difficult to imagine their parents engaged in sexual activity. Even though they know, in fact, it occurs, they find it difficult to imagine the scene. This inability is a natural tendency to try to repress sexual fantasies and feelings about parents. If you discuss your own sexual experiences with your child, you may make him anxious, since you will bring into the open something he finds more comfortable repressing. Moreover, your openness can unduly stimulate your child, which can have bad effects on his sexual attitudes and behavior, ranging anywhere from incestuous feelings to negative attitudes about sex in general. The most real danger involved in discussing your own sexual experiences with your child is that you may cause sexual arousal and perhaps feelings of resentment that can interfere with your child's normal and healthy sexual adjustment.

If my child knows about sex,
won't he want to experiment?

It is an absolute misconception to think that your child will take the sex information you give him and immediately put it to use. This misconception is prevalent because adults are inclined to project their own feelings into a child. Your child does not have the same sexual appetite that you do and is not yet motivated by the same hormones flowing through his system. His questions result from intellectual curiosity. He wants to understand the world better. Knowing about sex does not affect the degree of experimentation when it begins in the normal course of a child's emotional growth. In fact, many children who have no facts begin to experiment at the same time as their more informed friends.

Children become interested in their own bodies and in the bodies of other people. They become concerned about the similarities and differences, and they begin to wonder if other people get the same sensations they do. In fact, they examine each other's bodies as they play, and have been doing so for generations under the guise of "playing doctor." I often wonder how many people went into medicine because of frustrated desires to examine someone else's body.

Can it harm my child not to
know about sex?

Yes. Not knowing about reproduction and sex can be extremely harmful to your child, since it leaves him vulnerable to misinformation. He is also unprotected in situations involving sexual reactions that he will not know about. Ignorance in adolescence can lead to an unwanted pregnancy. You would be amazed to know how many adolescents engage in sexual play, even in sexual intercourse, without under-standing sex or reproduction. And you would be even more amazed at how many pregnancies occur because the girl does not know the danger of becoming pregnant when having intercourse. Contraceptive precautions are completely unthought-of by these youngsters because they are unheard-of.

Not telling a child about sex matters is analogous to not teaching your child about traffic regulations. No responsible parent would neglect teaching his child how to cross streets safely. This knowledge protects the child from getting killed by a passing truck. Similarly, not telling your child about sex leaves him absolutely vulnerable to a damaging experience. There is much documentation indicating that adolescents have been sexually molested because they were not aware of what was happening. As a matter of fact, approaching adoles-cence uninformed about and unprepared for sex can lead to damages that might be more ravaging than those sustained in a traffic accident.

The absence of information about sex and reproduction can be dangerous in another way. Your child may begin to develop fears because he has sexual reactions or physiological reactions that he doesn't understand or know anything about. Time and time again I have seen severe anxiety reactions when a girl begins menstruation without having been told what this means. As far as she's concerned, something serious has gone wrong in her body. After all, how else can she explain a spontaneous flow of blood from within her body if she does not have any prior concept of menstruation? Boys who have not been told about "wet dreams" may feel acutely embarrassed and at the same time panic-striken, wondering what's wrong with them. Boys' erections and girls' vaginal sensations and clitoral pleasures can be very perplexing to a growing child if he doesn't understand what these sensations mean. "Knowledge is strength." Your child will be much better prepared to cope with potential problem situations, and in particular sexual feelings, if he has been told the facts.

Chapter VIII

❁❀❁❀❁❀❁❀❁❀❁❀❁❀❁❀

Sex Experience

*When does my child begin to
experience sex?*

That depends to a large extent on what you define as a sex experience. Many psychoanalytic writers, particularly Freudians, include as sex experiences all stimulation as it occurs in infancy, and anal functions as they occur some time in the second and third year of life. While this definition may sound strange to some people and be hard to accept, there is reason to believe that the gratification an infant receives in conjunction with sucking behavior is related to the relaxation an adult experiences after sexual satisfaction.

However, for the purpose of our discussion, I prefer to consider sex experience as beginning when sensations from the male or female genitals become pleasant, usually some time during your child's third year. While a child is capable of some sexual arousal even earlier, the actual experience usually occurs inadvertently. Sometimes a parent changing a diaper accidentally stimulates a little boy and finds that he gets an erection and seems generally aroused when this occurs. Sometimes when a little girl is bounced on her parent's knee she is stimulated, experiences some clitoral sensations, and begins to show pelvic thrusts. These are normal

97

responses to inadvertent genital stimulation which occur automatically. Of course, a young child does not have the same fantasies or sexual appetites that an adult has when sexually aroused.

The more sophisticated sexual sensations that occur during the third year are related to your child's tendency to explore his own body. While he is exploring his body, if he inadvertently stimulates his genitals, the resulting pleasureful sexual sensation reinforces his tendency to continue to create sexual arousal the same way. This type of sexual arousal is a physiological reaction, not a response to sexual ideas.

When will my child begin to
masturbate?

Generally speaking, your child will begin to masturbate as soon as he grasps the relationship between stimulating his genitalia with his hands and the pleasureful result. This happens soon after he has enough muscular control to place his hands wherever he wants, but it usually does not occur with any frequency until a child is somewhere near the age of four. Episodes of self-stimulation that occur around bedtime or when a child is preoccupied with listening to a story or watching TV are common. Incidentally, if a child is left alone for long periods of time, and if he does not receive frequent stimulation from contacts with other people, his tendency to engage in self-stimulation may cause him to masturbate.

Is masturbation harmful?

Believe it or not, some people still think it is. It isn't. It is a natural phenomenon that begins in childhood and continues with varying frequency depending on many factors. Almost all, if not all, people have masturbated. Masturbation becomes quite common during adolescence and can persist through adulthood. Interestingly, many open-minded adults who discuss sex openly are hesitant to discuss masturbation, perhaps because most people associate masturbation with a feeling of guilt. Whether this is an inborn tendency or whether it results from subtle little hints by parents is hard to determine.

Masturbation gets to be a problem most frequently if a parent places great emphasis on it and takes a clearly punitive attitude when it occurs. The child reacts by feeling extremely guilty. He learns that he is engaging in a forbidden activity whenever he masturbates. This feeling of guilt can be generalized to any sexual situation, a bad omen for future sex relationships.

How should I react to my child's masturbation?

Be somewhat casual about it. Let him know in an offhand way that you know he masturbates, and then ignore the situation as much as possible. Of course, if he masturbates excessively, you will have to react more noticeably. But when you react to frequent or excessive masturbation, do not take a punitive attitude, or try to instill feelings of guilt, or threaten your child's self-esteem. Simply let him know that you are aware of his tendency to frequent self-stimulation. Since it is the fact of your reacting that is important, you can limit yourself to saying, "If you want to do what you're doing, why don't you go off and do it by yourself?" Or you might say, "I guess it feels good, but why do you do it so often?"

Many people do not agree, but I feel it is a mistake to ignore excessive masturbation, because your child may feel more anxious if you do not react. Recently I encountered a mother who was very proud of the fact that she never said one word to her child who masturbates so excessively that she has a vaginal irritation requiring medical attention. This mother's pride was based upon her notion that she must do nothing that might cause her child to feel guilty. It was my impression after getting to know this youngster that she was extremely anxious, largely because of her mother's greatly permissive attitude. I suggested to this mother that she suggest to her daughter that rubbing herself so much caused irritations and that for that reason she ought to try to control herself somewhat. Furthermore, I suggested that the mother tell her child that if she really wants to rub herself it would be more appropriate when she is not in public. When the mother followed my suggestion, there was a marked diminution in the youngster's anxiety and a marked decrease in her masturbation.

Looked at another way, your child may engage in masturbation openly and excessively with the secret hope that someone will set limits on what is considered socially acceptable. If you do not react, you are accepting this behavior without any reservations. Thus, I encourage you to react, but not punitively and not in a way which your child will feel as rejection.

Is it harmful for my child to
masturbate with other children?

It is perfectly natural for children to engage in sexual exploration activities. They may get to the point where they engage in "mutual masturbation." There is no intrinsic harm in children masturbating together except the slim possibility that it might become sufficiently satisfying for the child to show a marked preference for this kind of sexual stimulation. Then his preference tends to retard further sexual growth.

If your child is emotionally healthy, the likelihood is that the mutual masturbation experience will be transitory and that he will have no profound interest in continuing this activity. However, if you have an unhappy child who has experienced psychic trauma, anxiety, and emotional frustration, it is just possible that this kind of group sex play will constitute the most pleasurable sensation life has ever provided. If that is the case, your child will obviously and sensibly want to repeat the experience and continue this kind of satisfaction. Unusual forms of sexual activity generally develop and perpetuate themselves in this fashion.

There are so many things in life and in personality development that force a child to move ahead in his mastery of life's problems that there is little chance that your child will develop a fixation on any of these experiences unless there has previously been intense trauma or intense frustration. Thus, if you notice your child masturbating with other children, you should attempt to convey the idea that it is unacceptable in the same way you would if excessive masturbation were the problem.

What other childhood sex experiences occur?

Playing doctor seems to be a universal childhood sex experience. Almost any child who has ever visited a doctor seems to associate this with satisfying some degree of sexual curiosity. Children do examine each other's genitalia and "take each other's temperature." Most children get the idea that this is a forbidden activity and play doctor when their parents are not around. The unusual procedure involves taking down pants and looking at bottoms. They may use pencils or other obejcts to take temperatures. Usually the game does not involve any device penetrating the body, though it does occur. Sometimes children simply play "I'll show you mine if you show me yours."

When children have this experience, it satisfies their curiosity and allows them to explore each other's bodies, a significant step forward from self-stimulation. In many ways, playing doctor is probably the forerunner of heterosexual activity and, for better or worse, it has no relationship whatsoever to anything that the American Medical Association ever had in mind for certifying physicians. I hasten to add, however, that this game *can* lead to a fascination for "doing what a doctor does." This theory does not make me particularly popular with my colleagues who are physicians.

Playing doctor is not the only sexual exploration. Other

forms occur. Children can play with members of the same sex or members of the opposite sex. Sometimes the game leads to mutual masturbation, or to more complicated versions of sexual exploration. Although I am inclined to accept this type of exploration as normal behavior, I urge you to show your children that you are aware of their activities. React as you would to excessive masturbation, but don't be surprised if, in spite of your attitude, your child continues his sexual exploration. Actually, by creating a mild forbidden attitude, you may intensify your child's pleasure and perhaps encourage the idea that sexual pleasure, sexual activity, and sexual stimulation have some special significance in life. After all, it does.

One last point. I am inclined to discourage exploratory activity between members of the same sex. In fact, I urge you to minimize the possibility of its occurring simply because a child's first experience involving intense sexual satisfaction can have a marked influence on his ultimate sexual adaptation. I am inclined to believe that, all things being equal, if your child finds satisfaction with the same sex in his initial activities, there is a tendency to repeat the experience and the particular type of activity may become usual. In short, if you want to avoid the possible hazards of a homosexual adjustment, take a more relaxed view of heterosexual experiences and a more disapproving stance toward sexual stimulation that involves members of the same sex.

Should I tell my child that there
are sexually abnormal people?

Most definitely. I think you should explain to your child, but with considerable caution, that there are some people who feel differently about sex and that some of them are "sort of like sick people." In describing them it is helpful to mention that they were not born that way but became that way because of some bad experiences in their lives. Point out that they are not necessarily dangerous people but are rather misguided. As a matter of general information, sexually abnormal people are often abnormal because they were misinformed about sex when they were young, as numerous case histories show. You can say that these sick people may sometimes show their genitals to other people; you can indicate that some of them are more interested in members of their own sex than in members of the other sex; you may indicate that there are some older people who like to play with younger children, to undress them and play with their genitalia. In short, give your child some idea of the gamut of possibilities.

When you tell your child about abnormal people, be sure you present this information in objective terms. Emphasize an understanding of these people. Do not terrorize your child about a possible encounter with a disturbed person. And do not indicate in any way that violence or social ostracism will result. It is easy to traumatize any child simply by offering specific and detailed information about what sexually abnormal people might do. Don't. You might end up having a child who is so upset that he won't even want to go out on the street to go to school.

What can I do to prevent my
child from being disturbed by
an encounter with a sexually
disturbed adult?

There is very little that you can do. Fortifying your child with knowledge is perhaps the only way you can prepare him for a possible encounter with a sexually abnormal person. If you avoid explaining to your child that sexually abnormal people exist, and he then encounters such an individual, he will be defenseless against the possible ravages of this experience.

What do I do if something
unpleasant happens to my
child?

There is very little you can do except give your child as much support, reassurance, and acceptance as you can, while giving him every opportunity to talk about what happened. Try to get him to talk when he is emotionally aroused because of his trauma. It is the best time to offer reassurance. Tell your child he has had an unusual experience, which happens very, very infrequently. This is an actual fact. The impression many people have that abnormal sexual encounters are a frequent occurrence results from the fact that they are often recounted on the front page of the newspaper. Letting your child discuss the situation with you in detail gives you the chance to help him recognize that he had no direct responsibility for what occurred. This is important, because a child who has had such an experience is often afraid that his parents will feel that he initiated it.

Hopefully you have prepared your child for experiences like this. If not, you will be dealing with two difficult situations simultaneously: explaining to your child that some people are sexually abnormal and comforting him because some sexually abnormal individual has assaulted him. The tremendous difficulty, if not impossibility, of doing both together reemphasizes the value of prior preparation.

If I tell my child about these
abnormal experiences, will he
anticipate having them?

Perhaps. Children invariably look upon any novel situation as a possible occurrence. In fact, one way children learn to deal with situations that have not occurred is to make them occur in fantasies and deal with them in that way. If your child does imagine an abnormal encounter and the real experience happens later on, he will have had the equivalent of prior experience. In my opinion, the possibility that your child may anticipate an unpleasant experience and try to ease his anxiety by dealing with the frightening aspects in fantasy is no reason to avoid telling him that abnormal encounters sometimes occur.

Will my child have any sex
experiences which involve me?

Usually the first experience your child will have which can be interpreted in any way as involving you occurs when he sees you undressed. While it is not necessarily a sex experience at first, seeing parents nude may become one later on. Often children have no sexual interpretation for an experience when it occurs. Eventually, when they reach sexual maturity, their prior experiences recur in fantasy and are then embodied with some sexual connotation. Thus, seeing his parents going about without clothes may have no particular significance to a growing child other than teaching him the anatomy of the opposite sex. But later, when his own sexual feelings begin to develop, he may have some sexual feelings in conjunction with images of his naked parents. This sequence of events can upset your child.

Although aware of the problems, I am inclined to think that seeing you nude is a positive experience for a young child. Seeing you get in and out of a bath or a shower or changing clothes is perhaps the best way for your child to experience nudity. If you go around completely nude for long periods of time, your child might experience subsequent confusion. And while I encourage you to allow your children to see you naked, I caution you about being seductive, erotic, or in any way sexually provocative. The danger is that a child aroused by his parent of the opposite sex is very often inclined to inhibit his heterosexual feelings. Incidentally, while incestuous experiences are not a frequent occurrence, they are by no means unknown. Incest is prohibited by legal statutes to protect children from sexual abuse. There is good reason for these laws, because a direct sex experience between child and parent has devastating psychological effects. Unfortunately, it is possible for parents to be seductive with a child without engaging in any direct sexual activity. What happens is that the parent actually increases the intensity of the child's arousal, which is almost as devastating as direct sexual contact between parent and child.

Psychiatrists and psychologists know it is common for mothers and sons, as well as fathers and daughters, to develop strong affections that ultimately have some bearing on the child's sexual adaptation. If a child is unable to relinquish his ties with his parent of the opposite sex so that he may begin to express sexual feelings toward other members of the opposite sex, obvious problems result. Confused ties occur most frequently when there are marital frictions and a parent may be inclined to exploit his relationship with a child for his own emotional needs. For example, an unhappy wife might easily derive undue satisfaction from her contact with her son and in the process unconsciously convey sexual connections. Obviously, when this happens, her child is more apt to demonstrate sexual aberrations in later life.

Should I let my child get into
my bed?

One of the early experiences your child has that may cause some feeling of sexual arousal or may possibly have sexual connotations later on is being taken into your bed. Psychoanalysts have been very firm in their recommendation that parents should *never* allow children into their beds. Although there may be some virtue in this recommendation, my experience tells me that very few parents are able to abide by this rule in an absolute fashion, and I cannot take the position that it should "never" occur. It is perhaps more realistic to explain to your child that he has his own bed and really ought to sleep there.

If your child does come to your bed, perhaps when he needs reassurance in the night, the event does not necessarily mean that he will damage the relationship between his parents or that it will constitute a psychic trauma. Of course, you should avoid any possibility of direct sexual stimulation and should terminate it if your child initiates it. Most important of all, you should not allow him to interfere with the intimacy of the relationship between husband and wife. If your child becomes accustomed to coming into your bed, his habit will inhibit sexual activity between you and your spouse and can be a source of resentment. Allowing a child to be a wedge between husband and wife may be momentarily pleasing to the child, but in the long run it creates difficulties for him in establishing a healthy sexual identity. If your child feels that he can be a wedge between his parents, he will be less inclined to identify with the parent of the same sex. After all, that same-sexed parent has permitted himself to be pushed aside.

Is it natural for my child to inquire about my sexual activity?

Yes. A child begins to wonder whether his parents engage in sexual activities as soon as he knows about sex and reproduction. If you have been casual and open in talking about sex, your child may directly inquire whether you have intercourse, and how often.

How do I handle that question?

The only way is to tell your child that this is a private matter, not open for discussion. Remind him that sexual experiences do have a personal and private quality. In fact, they are regarded as so private that not even members of the family are permitted to discuss them. If the question is asked by a very young child, you may be able to deal with it superficially. If you are dealing with an adolescent, you may want to refer him to literature on the subject to give him some ideas of the sexual norms.

What if my child walks in while we are having intercourse?

You can't do anything but react. And how you react is important. I suspect you might feel a little like a child caught masturbating. You might even feel guilty, and then attempt to excuse your behavior. In short, a defensive reaction. But this is not the appropriate reaction. After all, are you doing anything to feel guilty about? If your initial reaction is "Please get out of here," it would be more appropriate and perhaps best for your child's emotional health.

The reason I recommend an aggressive reaction, but not, of course, a punitive or rejecting one, is that I think it wise to clearly establish the importance of privacy in matters of sex. Surprisingly, your child may feel guilty about interrupting you and be apologetic. You will continue to be embarrassed anyway and will have a difficult time knowing what to say. The tack I recommend is to explain how much you love each other and say that sometimes when you kiss someone, you sort of want to hold them close and get very, very excited when this happens. You want to have the experience of touching the other person, feeling them, and almost being part of the other person's body. It just may be possible at a time like this for you to convey the intensity of the feelings of love and its physical counterpart.

Psychiatrists and psychologists have long known that confusion can develop in your child's mind if he makes an association between aggression, violence, and sexual arousal. When you are engaged in sexual intercourse, your movements, your sounds, and your expressions can be interpreted by an innocent child as wrestling, fighting, or somehow hurting each other. For this reason, be somewhat discreet in your

sexual activities even when your children are infants because,
while infants and young children may not actually see you,
they may very well hear the sounds that you make. Your
heavy breathing, gasping, and perhaps moans and groans
may upset your child. If your adolescent child sees or hears
your sex relations, the reaction is different, since the average
adolescent knows about sex. He may be inclined to be aroused
sexually, which could be confusing to him later on.

The necessity of privacy for sex creates a dilemma, since
most parents allow children the privilege of moving freely in
and out of their bedroom. If this is true in your home, the
moment you lock the door your child, like any child, wants
to come in. His curiosity may become suspicion when at certain times, and only at certain times, the door is locked. It
works better to establish some rules of privacy that prevail,
regardless of your plans for sexual activity.

Chapter IX

ଡ଼ାଡ଼ାଡ଼ାଡ଼ାଡ଼ାଡ଼ାଡ଼ାଡ଼ାଡ଼ାଡ଼ାଡ଼ାଡ଼ାଡ଼ାଡ଼

Grandparents, Relatives, and Concerned Others

Should I encourage my child to
relate to individuals outside his
family?

Yes. It is important for your child to have a multitude of relationships with other people. But you should realize that these relationships are much more meaningful and productive if your child has first established a solid and secure relationship with you and others within your household. When he knows that you offer love, affection, and unconditional support in the face of any threat, strangers and relatives are good choices for increasing skills used in social interaction.

If your child is forced to meet many people and is indirectly pressured into relationships with all types of individuals when he does not feel supported by his own parents, these relationships can be threatening and confusing. Once threatened, your child may tend to withdraw, or worse, to look upon these external relationships with extreme caution and perhaps even cynicism.

*How soon does my child begin
to relate to persons outside the
family household?*

Although in the early weeks and months of life your child
may be relating to others without any particular conscious
awareness, outside relationships will not be as meaningful until
he is close to a year old and shows more capacity to realize
that other people are different. Actually, your child begins to
relate to persons outside the family whenever someone else
takes an active role in caring for him.

*What form do these early rela-
tionships take?*

Your child's early relationships are simple. He is curious
about people and aware that they are not his parents.
Strangely enough, your child will be selective around the
middle of his first year and will prefer those people who
provide stimulation on a level that satisfies his need, neither
ignoring him nor overwhelming him. Children rarely like
people who are aloof and pay no attention to them. By the
same token, children often react badly to people who come
on "strong," trying to excite them and get a reaction before
they have sized up the visitor. A child wants to satisfy his
initial curiosity, which most likely involves recognizing the
difference between people he is familiar with and new people
he does not know. Most of all, the sense of trust or distrust
that your child has learned from you will affect his relationships with everyone else. If he trusts you, he will be inclined
to trust others.

*Why does my child say,
"Danny's mother says so and
so"?*

The likelihood is that your child is trying to get you to do
something that Danny's mother has done with Danny or

allowed Danny to do. Do not be easily influenced by this technique. You should make clear to your child that Danny's mother does not tell you what to do. Then your child will grow to understand that what applies in one situation is not always applicable in another.

Incidentally, it wouldn't hurt to recognize that parents use the same tactics, which is usually where your child got the idea. You say "Look at the way Danny helps his mother" or "Look at the way Danny eats his dinner" or "Look at the way Danny does his homework"—"Why can't you be like Danny?" Clearly, any child noticing this kind of parental comparison might compare his mother with Danny's mother. Avoid making comparisons so that you do not get caught up in this kind of dilemma. Make it clear that Danny is Danny and "You are you." Point out that neither of them should be used as a comparison for the other.

Don't children constantly make comparisons anyway?

Not really. If you constantly make or allow comparisons between children, you are encouraging competition and undermining your child's feelings of individuality. If you constantly compare him with another child, he usually gets the idea that you like the other child more than you like him. Moreover, he feels his behavior never satisfies you. After all, why do you always like what the other child does? As the old proverb says, "Comparisons are odious." I agree.

Will my child like his relatives?

Maybe. But he will not automatically like his relatives any more than he would automatically like anyone else. The chances are that your child will be apprehensive at first while he formulates feelings and attitudes based upon how his relatives act toward him. Most children are sensitive to others' reactions. Often they adopt an attitude that conforms to your attitude. If you like your relatives, your child will most likely like them, too. Likewise, if you hate your relatives. Luckily, relatives are inclined, particularly when they grow up, to deal with members of their own families with an extra degree of indulgence and acceptance. Any child generally responds. Therefore, your child may very well have a special attitude and a special set of feelings about his relatives, but these feelings are not based on the fact that these people are biological "blood relatives."

Grandparents hold a unique position in your child's life. They usually have a great sense of pride in a grandchild and are demonstrative and affectionate. Grandparents enjoy reliving their own experiences with their own children and have the unique advantage of being free to withdraw from the scene whenever the going gets rough. They can turn over the less pleasant tasks of child rearing to you. Consequently, grandparents are labeled indulgent because they enjoy "spoiling" your child. They fully believe they have earned the right to indulge their grandchildren. They like the admiration with which their happy grandchildren acknowledge their indulgence. And your child loves every minute of it. This mutual admiration society may discomfort you, but since each of us is a potential grandparent, I am not inclined to put down this special relationship. Your child enjoys it, his grandparents are revitalized, and the perplexed, irritated parent should accept it.

*Then should I foster my child's
relationship with his grandparents?*

Absolutely, yes. I feel that a young child should get to know people of different ages and understand the kinds of problems and reactions older people have. For example, your child may be surprised when he finds that his grandparent is unable to get down on all fours to play without showing some discomfort. Seeing this gives your child some under-standing about the aging process and about the differences between people of different ages. These are important lessons for your child to learn. In our culture we are unfortunately inclined to keep children together and away from older peo-ple, a policy that can only lead to misunderstandings and insensitiveness.

Are there no disadvantages?

The only disadvantages I know of arise if grandparents create conflict between you and your child. Because grand-parents have had the experience of raising your child's par-ents, they sometimes feel more knowledgeable than you. They may make you feel inadequate. Grandparents should realize that they themselves had the opportunity of raising children their own way and that you deserve the same chance. They can and should enjoy their grandchildren without interfering with the methods and procedures you use in raising your child. Of course, it is nice if they are available to offer assist-ance and advice when asked.

If there is going to be conflict, it usually involves breaking rules. Grandparents often undermine the discipline and limits you set. For example, you may decide to give your child a weekly allowance to teach him to deal with money. Then his grandparents come along fully prepared to indulge him and ingratiate themselves. They give your child small sums of money to spend on whatever he wants. Obviously, this indul-gence pleases your child, since he can buy some things he might otherwise not have. But by providing the immediate gratification his grandparents have undermined your attempt to teach your child how to cope with one of life's problems. It is just possible that the well-meaning grandparents are making this little gift to satisfy their own needs. They like the pleasure resulting from the child's satisfaction at receiving the gift.

*Should I force my child to
make presents for his grandparents?*

No. I don't think you will teach your child to like or respect his grandparents if you force him into a relationship with them by making him make presents. But I think you can easily hint to your child that his grandparents might be very pleased and happy to receive a present that he made. You can safely encourage your child to make something, since your child's reward is sure to be nothing short of a happy, smiling, and proud grandparent.

*Is the interaction between my
child and his grandparents
important enough to warrant
trips to see them?*

Absolutely. Any trip is always stimulating for your child, particularly because he will enjoy the anticipation and dream about the pleasures he will have when he arrives. Sometimes your child's excitement overwhelms him and causes tears and frustration. But the knowledge that grandparents exist and that you are planning a special trip to visit them is a thrilling adventure. Incidentally, nothing is more pleasing to grandparents than a visit from grandchildren who love them, worship them, and enjoy all the indulgences they shower on them. Children remember with great intensity the happy emotions and pleasant times grandparents have had with them. Unfortunately, many children also become unhappy and anxious when they see grandparents who are ill or handicapped. Nevertheless, your youngster should have the chance to share in their lives.

*Why do grandparents seem to
want to spoil my child?*

Grandparents have had the experience of raising their own children, with all the pleasures and headaches involved in child rearing. As they get on in years and look forward with an understandable sense of pride to another generation of descendants, they try to express their pleasure and share their pleasure by giving their grandchild everything he wants and all the things you have decided not to give him. My advice is to deal with this situation by telling your child that "While grandma and grandpa give you whatever you want, I don't want you to get the idea that I will, too." You are not being cruel, and your child will not interpret it in that way, either. He does learn very quickly to exploit the indulgent attitude of his grandparents and at the same time often respects you more if you do not compete with them to see who can ingratiate himself fastest. Maintain your discipline and your values. Show your child that you will not be conned into doing what his grandparents do. I might add, I don't think grandparents really want to "spoil" their grandchildren. I think they simply want to have all the advantages of parenthood without any of the disadvantages. Perhaps this is a right they fall heir to when they achieve grandparenthood.

Will grandparents' presents
actually harm my child?

No, provided these gifts are not supposed to interfere with your relationship with your child. If you have expressed a strong and firm attitude about what your child should not have, and if his grandparents turn around and give him what you have prohibited, the grandparents are plainly and simply undermining your relationship with your child.

Situations so potentially damaging can usually be avoided if there is communication among all involved. The crucial point to bear in mind is that you have to be acknowledged by grandparents as primarily responsible for your child. The moment any other figure poaches on your prime responsibility, problems begin to develop. Perhaps you can maintain the close communication with grandparents which will permit you to help them select presents they know will be useful for your child and which will fit into the value system you have set up in your family. If you are skillful, you can do this without blunting the good wishes and feelings grandparents want to express by indulging their grandchildren.

How shall I tell my child he
must get on with members of
the family?

As all of us know, you can pick your friends, but you cannot pick your relatives. It's sometimes hard to explain this to your child, particularly when you want to maintain good relations with relatives, even though these relatives have personalities you would not tolerate among acquaintances. Your best approach is to avoid forcing your child to accept members of the family whom he does not like. On occasion this tactic creates difficulty if you have a particular reason for maintaining diplomatic relations with one member of your family. But if you organize a set of double standards for your child, one for friends and one for relatives, you can confuse him. Apply the same standards for friends as you do for relatives, at least at first. Later, when your child is able to understand the finer nuances of social relationships, you can explain that while you may not like certain relatives, there are extenuating circumstances for preserving friendly relationships with them.

Will my child know I dislike
some of my spouse's relatives?

It is extremely hard to hide your real feelings from your child. Even at a very young age, he will pick up cues about feelings you may be trying to hide. He may even embarrass you by his sensitive awareness of your feelings. Thus, if you do not like your in-laws, your child will most likely know it.

Perhaps the best way to deal with your feelings of dislike, for your in-laws or for that matter for anyone else, is to tell your child about your feelings and give him the honest option of liking the same person you dislike. He may, after all. And if you allow him his opinion without making him feel guilty for feeling differently from you, you will be teaching him a significant lesson. You will be teaching him that it is possible to disagree amicably. In addition, you are recognizing your child as an individual and showing respect for his feelings. Of course, you should help your child recognize his own feelings and express them even if they are different from yours. For some strange reason many parents feel that a child should show a sense of loyalty toward all the same things they do. I don't.

One of my friends, a school-
teacher with a great deal of
training in child psychology,
constantly proffers corrective
advice. Should I follow it?

It is always advisable to take other people's advice with a grain of salt. Advice is easily given. Help involves something more. In any case, I think you have the right to make your own mistakes. Get as much knowledge as you can, and make some attempt to apply it sensibly and efficiently. Don't blindly follow other people's advice. There are too many people around who like to manipulate others and do so simply by sounding authoritative and knowledgeable. By now you know I would like you to follow your own instincts and judgment. A teacher may or may not have the special qualities for being a good parent. Remember he or she is an expert in teaching children, not necessarily in meeting the emotional needs of your child.

I must say that I have treated numerous problem children whose mothers have been schoolteachers. I think the reason may be that these mothers continue being schoolteachers while raising their children. They forget to be mothers. Likewise, a psychologist or psychiatrist may treat his child as an emotionally disturbed person or potential neurotic. This parent tends to overexplain an ordinary situation in more detail than necessary. He attempts to keep his child from feeling anxious. But the child gets the idea that life is potentially traumatizing. Unconsciously, he complies with his parent's expectations and does become disturbed.

My own children at times accuse me of being overbearing and demanding by saying, "You are a child psychologist—you are supposed to understand children, not punish them." I invariably reply, "You're right. I am a child psychologist, but to other children. To you, I am a father. My disciplining you is part of my responsibility as your father." What all of this means is that children must have mothers and fathers who are parents, not teachers or psychologists or psychiatrists.

Chapter X

Doctors, Medicines,
and Illness

*Why are children apprehensive
about doctors?*

They learn to be. Children are not afraid of doctors at first; in fact, they may even be fascinated by them. The doctor does various intriguing things to them. He uses equipment that nobody else has and generally engages in activities that make a child curious. A child's apprehension usually starts when it becomes appropriate to feel apprehensive—when the doctor begins to do things that are unpleasant. Having strange instruments stuck in his ears, nose, and mouth, being pricked with needles, and having someone poking around where it sometimes hurts is not only unpleasant, it is an infringement of privacy and an intrusion upon free will. Sometimes, too, the doctor's examination frightens a child because the situation is strange. If the child were more familiar with what was going on, he would be less scared.

I consider it natural for your child to object to some things the doctor does. If you or the doctor criticize him because he is unwilling to allow the doctor to continue his activities without some objection, you are not accepting your child's feelings. I don't mean that your child has to like what is going on, but you should recognize that the child does have feelings and furthermore that these feelings are extremely appropriate indeed. Your child should be helped with his discomfort and apprehension and not made to feel he is wrong to object. He will eventually learn, and I think it is important for you to convey this message, that there are many things in life one must do even though one doesn't like doing them. It is easier for anyone to accept this unpleasant truth when there is someone around who understands your feelings. Ask yourself how you'd like it if a stranger examined every orifice of your body despite your objections.

*How can I help my very young
child deal with unpleasant
treatment in a doctor's office?*

It is difficult to do so because you really can't prepare a child for such an experience until he is between a year and a year and a half old. He is not yet enough aware to understand the doctor's function and will react largely to what is done to him. If it is pleasant, it is acceptable. if it is unpleasant, it is bad. Since what the doctor does is generally more unpleasant than pleasant, it is obvious that your child will react accordingly.

Since you can't prepare an infant or young baby for a physical examination or some other unpleasant medical procedure, you can at least buffer the unpleasantness by offering your child some emotional support. Infants and babies usually respond positively to being held and cuddled when they are unhappy. This is about all you can do. Communicate sympathy in any way you can. Reduce the unpleasantness of the experience as much as you can. Distraction is probably the most helpful tool. For this reason, lollipops are very useful in the armamentarium of the pediatrician.

*How can I help my older child
deal with a visit to the doctor?*

The best way you can help an older child is to prepare him for what he is about to encounter. Your child is ready to be told what to expect when he is old enough to understand some words and knows the difference between *now* and *later*. The child must be able to understand that you are talking about something that will occur. A young child who doesn't understand words and cannot be talked to may begin to scream as soon as he sees the familiar waiting room and that scary white coat, since even before a young child can talk, he can make associations. Children as young as eight months react with overt fear and hysteria when seeing the doctor's waiting room, or for that matter, anyone in a white coat. The intensity of the reaction, of course, depends on the child's previous experience. The more painful the experience, the greater the fear. Obviously, you can prepare your child best if you have full knowledge about what he will encounter. If you do not, preparation is still important for the child who can understand. He should not be brought into a doctor's office without having been told something in advance.

What do I tell my child about going to the doctor?

Tell him the truth. This is the cardinal rule in preparing your child for any medical procedure. If your child is going to have an injection, tell him, "You are going to have an injection, and it is probably going to hurt; if you want to cry, that's all right, because when something hurts, it may make you cry." Following this preparation, if your child has his injection and cries, you can take an understanding attitude by saying, "Yes, I know it hurts—that's why you're crying." Then you can comfort your child. However, if your child has the injection and doesn't cry, you have put yourself in a position to say, "My, you were very brave—I know it hurt and you didn't even cry."

When you prepare your child this way, that is, honestly, you cannot harm him. If your child handles the situation bravely, you can tell him so. Your praise will enhance his self-esteem and will help him deal with the next similar situation. If he cries, you will have predicted a response that did occur. At least he has faced an unpleasant situation, had an appropriate response, has received your support, and has not lost face. No matter which reaction your child has, you have given him the opportunity for mastering a situation, but most important, you were honest with him. He will remember your honesty and will continue to trust you.

If you are not sure what your child will encounter during a visit to the doctor, make some attempt to find out, so you can tell your child about it in advance. If you can't find out, don't act as if you know and try to fabricate. Your child will sense your ignorance and be apprehensive simply because he recognizes your uncertainty. Most children eventually get to understand and accept the fact that you may not know what is going to happen. Your simple statement, "Frankly, I don't know what the doctor will do," will be accepted as an honest preparation.

Unfortunately, the procedure that most parents employ has the opposite effect. A parent tells his child, "This isn't going to hurt a bit." Then the child is given an injection that does indeed hurt. He begins to cry. His tears may be the result of pain, but are enriched by feelings of anger, fury, and disappointment. Often the misguided parent compounds the mistake by asking, "What are you crying for? I told you it didn't even hurt." Needless to say, the parent is literally adding insult to injury. His remark implies that the child is overreacting, that he is a failure, that he wasn't brave enough to withstand something that wasn't even painful. Clearly, the parent makes the child lose face.

In actual fact, the parent who takes this approach has lied to his child by telling him the injection would not hurt. He tries to cover up his lie by trying to make the child feel as if he, the child, has failed. The person who handles the situation in this way has totally disregarded the child's feelings and his potential for mastering this threatening situation.

This approach, I am sorry to say, is too often employed by doctors, nurses, and hospitals.

What happens if my child is
unprepared or misinformed?
He learns very quickly that you do not have his best interests at heart, that you do not protect him, and that you are a "liar." Once you have deceived your child, you have lost his trust. You will never entirely undo the damage. You can see now why some children begin to shriek, scream, and disbelieve whatever their parents tell them.

Some parents and doctors are hesitant about telling a child the truth about an unpleasant medical procedure because they fear that the child may become angry and resist. Even if it is necessary to hold your child down, it is still best to tell him the truth. Your child does not have to like what is happening, but he must accept it. This is a very important lesson for each of us to learn, since we all encounter many things in the course of our existence that we must put up with in spite of our dislike.

The properly prepared child—even if he did not believe you, or if he did and cried afterward—may continue to be apprehensive about doctors. But at least he will trust you and listen very carefully the next time he is told what may happen.

When should I begin my prepa-
ration for a visit to the doctor?
A short time before the visit. If you begin telling your child about it days in advance, his anxiety may build enormously with the help of his fantasies. He will be overwhelmed by his expectations and perhaps immobilized by his fears. A "short time before" does not mean on the threshold of the doctor's office, nor on your way in the car. Let your child know of the impending visit about a half-day in advance.

While it is important to prepare your child, I think it is equally important to avoid overpreparation. If you show deep concern and adopt a serious, possibly morose, attitude, your child will sense that something that requires this kind of preparation must be something extremely serious and dangerous. You will make him anxious and suddenly find that your child begins to conform with your attitude, feels he is facing something very major, and becomes afraid. Repeatedly, I have seen parents do this. They mean well and are trying to help their child, but they are actually increasing the child's anxiety and making an unpleasant situation more unpleasant than it actually is.

What I mean is this: If your child is about to have blood taken from his finger, it would be appropriate to deal with that situation in a matter-of-fact way. Say, "Johnny, the doctor must take some blood from your finger for a test—it may hurt but he will do it very quickly and get it over with." If you say to your child, "Johnny, come here, I want to talk to you about something—please sit down for a moment. I have something unpleasant to tell you, and I don't want you to be frightened—" you are probably overdoing it. That preparation alone would make most children extremely anxious.

What can I do if my child has
been misled by my doctor?

Once your child has been misled about medical procedures by a doctor or by anyone else, it is very difficult to regain his confidence. The doctor who misleads your child will on subsequent visits find him distrustful and resistant. This reaction can have unfortunate long-range implications for your child's health. After all, if he learns not to trust doctors, the child patient may as an adult be disinclined to consult a doctor when there is ample reason to do so. Subsequently, he could find that he has neglected a serious medical problem that could have been prevented had he had more confidence in his doctor.

If a doctor misleads your child, do not take sides with the doctor. If you do, you weaken your child's confidence in you by defending a doctor your child sees as dishonest. Perhaps the best way to deal with the situation is to educate doctors, particularly pediatricians, about the implications of their techniques for dealing with children.

How can I help my child cope with pain?

When you anticipate that your child will experience pain, let him know you understand that he may want to cry when something hurts. Let him know you understand this expression of discomfort. Do not make him feel that he is weak or a "baby." Let him know that you comprehend how unpleasant the pain must be, and offer him praise for being brave when you see him tolerating discomfort. By focusing on understanding his feelings, you will contribute to his sense of self-esteem. And you will be teaching him to adapt to life's stresses.

Another technique can be very helpful. Give your child some control over the painful situation and let him feel that he has some choice in the matter. You can ask him, "Would you like your injection while you're standing up or sitting down?" or "Would you like it in this arm or that arm?" or "Would you like a green lollipop or a red one?" These choices may seem relatively unimportant to you but they give your child the feeling that he is participating in his fate. Giving your child a choice notifies him that you are concerned about him. Even though you are asking him to undergo something unpleasant, you still want to make it as agreeable as possible. After all, he is not in the position to choose whether the treatment will be done or not. This choice has been made for him. So, at least give him the opportunity of choosing within reasonable limits how it is to be done. If your child refuses to make the choice, you will have to make it for him. But even then you have conveyed the idea that you were concerned with his feelings and are on record as having given him a chance.

What do I tell my child when
he has to take medicine?

If your doctor has prescribed medicine that you must administer to your child, you may have the task of giving your child something he doesn't like. If the medicine is to be given by mouth, he may not like the taste. If the medicine is eyedrops, eardrops, or a suppository, you simply have to tell your child that this is something that the doctor wants him to take so that he can get well. I advise you not to say, "Do it for your mother [or father]—it will make me so happy," or "If you take your medicine, I will give you a toy."

I am opposed to offering rewards for compliance because it undermines your child's chance to master an unpleasant situation. You are contributing to the idea that he should be rewarded by some gift for every unpleasant situation. It is far better for your child to learn to cope with these situations and to discover the sense of strength that follows being able to do something unpleasant. Alternatively, if you imply that he should take his medicine for his mother or his father, you are introducing the idea that he may be rejected if he doesn't. This approach can have detrimental psychological effects. For instance, you may find that your child uses taking medicine to find emotional satisfaction. If he feels unloved or unwanted, or if he has been taught to get his parents to cajole him into taking medicine in exchange for their love, he may do just that, use supposed illness to get your support.

What shall I do about giving
my infant medicine?

Just give it to him as quickly and painlessly as possible. If your baby resists, you may have to force the medicine into him. Even though this is unpleasant for your infant or baby, it is most unlikely you will do any irreparable damage psychologically, particularly if you comfort him immediately afterward. Incidentally, there are two schools of thought about whether you should hold your child while the doctor is giving him an injection, looking into his ears, or proceeding with some other intrusion. If you hold your child, he may feel comforted. On the other hand, your child may feel betrayed. After all, why don't you stop these unpleasantnesses and take him away? The ultimate choice is yours. I can see advantages and disadvantages either way.

I have often wondered why pediatricians don't give parents a disposable plastic syringe (without the needle, of course) when they have to give medication orally to an infant. The medication can be drawn into the syringe, the syringe placed in the corner of the child's mouth, and the medication ejected through the syringe. This technique would seem easier than trying to get a spoon filled with unpleasant-tasting medication into a young child's mouth. Expedient methods such as this should be relied upon as much as possible to decrease your child's trauma.

What do I do if my older child refuses medication?

You should make some attempt to reason with him. Be sure to acknowledge that you accept his feelings of distaste and make things as easy for him as you can. Don't hesitate to offer candy, syrup, or anything else that may help disguise the taste. In the end, though, let your child know that he must take the medicine, that that's the way the world is, and no one always has all things the way he wants them. Under no circumstances should you try to embarrass your child into taking the medication or make him feel that he is a baby because he is unwilling or hesitant. You will have more luck if you accept his feelings. It always helps to be apologetic, to say you're sorry that it has to be done, but that it does have to be done.

What do I tell my child if he
has to go to the hospital?

That depends to a large extent on what your child is going to the hospital for and his condition when he goes. Generally speaking, a child who is acutely ill or who is in great discomfort, or who has a high fever, or who feels very "sick," usually shows little apprehension about entering a hospital. Nevertheless, the child requires preparation the same as a child going in for diagnostic tests. Even though your child may not appear to react, because he feels sick, he should have as much information as he is able to comprehend. Give him as honest an account as you can of what will occur. Honesty is equally important whether your child's problem is an infected hangnail or major surgery. I frequently encounter extremely disturbed youngsters who have come to a hospital without any preparation whatsoever. Obviously, the effects are disastrous. It is particularly important that your child be able to trust you at this time of crisis. If you have deceived him, your child will tend to cling to you, perhaps to overreact to any treatment, however minor. Once you have deceived a child, he understandably requires enormous amounts of reassurance. In fact, the reassurance a deceived child requires will seem almost limitless.

Another common problem I encounter involves a child whose parents have told him he is coming to the hospital for tests, when in fact he is coming for surgery. A specific instance occurred recently. A day and a half after the child was admitted, he was taken to the operating room for brain surgery. During the period of recovery he experienced severe anxiety caused by the misinformation given him as preparation for his hospital stay. His parents' misrepresentation left him totally without resources to cope with his trauma and without anyone he could rely upon and trust. While the child cried for his mother and wanted her all the time, he showed tremendous ambivalence toward her and was at the same time extremely hostile toward her. Needless to say, it was difficult for anyone to convince this child thereafter that he was being told the truth. In fact, he needed intensive post-operative medical treatment, which had to be delayed because of his agitated behavior and his vivid fear, all of which was detrimental to his health. We had to embark upon a regimen that involved telling this youngster precisely every single thing that was going to happen. Our hope was to dilute his unpleasant experience with a series of experiences involving predictions that came true. We hoped the upsetting experience would become less paramount in his mind. For example, we instructed his parents to tell him in advance when they were going to leave, how long they would be gone, and when they would return. We would then point out that these things actually happened.

How do I prepare my child for surgery?

Many hospitals today have programs that are set up specifically to prepare a child for an operation involving anesthesia. The purpose of this preparation, which is usually carried out by the nursing staff and generally involves some specialized training, is to give the child some prior knowledge of what he will encounter. It is meant to decrease his anxiety and to help engage the child and his own resources in a cooperative manner for all that lies ahead. The child is told, usually the day before surgery, very concretely what will take place, step by step. The most effective technique uses miniature equipment and dolls. The nurse is able to show the child how the anesthesia is administered with a mask, how injections are given. The child uses a toy syringe and injects a doll, usually a doll dressed as a nurse, which gives the child some satisfaction, at least unconsciously, and a way of getting back at the nurses for whatever discomfort they have caused. Small intravenous bottles and needles are sometimes used on the doll to show the child how he may get the liquid his body needs after the operation. Bandages and dressings are applied. The cooperation of the child is solicited by getting him to participate with the nurse in this preoperative doll play. The result of this whole procedure is that the child becomes familiar with what will happen so that he will be less traumatized psychologically.

Many children approach this preparatory doll play with little apprehensiveness and no particular reaction. Luckily, it is not necessary for the child to react emotionally to this preoperative teaching, but he must know what will happen, even though he is not particularly apprehensive about the surgical procedure. After the surgery, when the child is in pain, he will remember that the adults responsible for his care told him in advance what would happen. He will know that they can be trusted later on.

In your preoperative preparation, stress to your child that he will not be aware of the pain or feel anything during the operation because he will be asleep. If your child has not been prepared for surgery and learns later, as he surely will, that it all took place while he was asleep and without his prior knowledge, he quite likely will develop some apprehension, if not a full-blown fear, of going to sleep. After all, if something was cut off or cut out while he was asleep, something similar may happen the next time he goes to sleep.

Not all hospitals believe in preoperative teaching. In fact, most hospitals offer a child little, if any, preoperative preparation. If this is the case with your child, make doubly sure that he has some prior knowledge from you about what will happen. Find out as much as you can about the surgery that will take place, and tell your child as much as he can understand.

What else can I do to help a
child who is hospitalized?

The best thing you can do is to stay with him as much as you can. Give your child the feeling that you will not abandon

him and that you will be nearby to offer support in case anything painful occurs. At a time like this, it is helpful if you
can be available at mealtimes to help feed the child. And I
highly recommend your staying overnight in the hospital
with your child. It may be inconvenient for you, but it prevents psychological problems that are extremely difficult to
cure later. It is quite common for any child to have trouble
sleeping after being in the hospital, particularly if he was
separated from his parents most of the time. In short, take
care of your child as much as possible when he is in the
hospital.

Doctors and nurses frequently claim that children cry more
when their parents are around. They are right, but not
because, as they think, the parents make the child unhappy,
but because the child has learned that his parents usually
come to his rescue in the face of any threat. The crying is
meant to have the parents remove him from the threatening
hospital. A child quickly learns that the doctors and nurses
will not react the way his parents will. Consequently, he is
inclined to cry more when his parents are around. Nevertheless, some doctors and nurses, still assuming that parents
cause the crying, insist parents be kept away from the hospital. These doctors and nurses are wrong. It is ultimately best
for the child to be with his parents, even if the noise annoys
the medical staff.

Unfortunately, not all hospitals provide for parents to be
with their children. Worse yet, they do not even recognize
the parents' presence as an important factor in buffering the
trauma of being in a hospital. Thus, when you consider what
you can do to help your child if hospitalization is required,
find a hospital that acknowledges your child's need for his
parents and is willing to set up procedures to accommodate
children and parents. Every effort should be made to find the
kind of hospital that will provide for these needs, even if it
involves some inconvenience for you. At the same time, I

think it is important that your doctor should recognize the psychological needs of children. He should assist you in meeting them. Try to find one who will.

What are the feelings of a chronically ill or handicapped child?

Theoretically the feelings of these children should be no different from the feelings of any other child. While this is theoretically true, chronically ill or handicapped children often have different reactions to life in general. For example, a child requiring crutches, a brace, or a wheelchair will invariably be an object of curiosity to other children. This fact will increase the handicapped child's sense of self-consciousness beyond the norm. Moreover, children who have some handicap will find that other people are oversolicitous and that some people express great sympathy simply because of their handicap. It is obvious, therefore, that this can affect the handicapped child's personality and his reactions to life's situations.

One of the chief reasons the handicapped child's reactions are different from those of other children is his own parents' reactions to him. Remember, parental reactions are by far the most important element in the formulation of a child's feelings about himself and the world. Parents of chronically ill children can make the care of their children their life's work. This obviously causes a parent-child relationship that is different from what is normally the case. I do not mean to be critical of the parents of a chronically ill child, because their feelings are often quite appropriate. Perhaps you can best appreciate this by recognizing the difficulties these parents have in coping with their child's handicap and in coping with their own feelings of extra responsibility for their child. Take, for example, hemophiliacs. I have often heard complaints that it is difficult to deal with these sick children because of the "overanxiousness" of their parents. These parents are not, in my experience and in my opinion, *overanxious*. They are *appropriately* anxious. After all, if you had a child who bled as a result of a minor bruise and whose uncontrolled bleeding episodes caused him great discomfort, possibly even irreparable damage, you too would be inclined to take many added precautions and be constantly on guard against any possible injury. Parents with this kind of problem are anxious, the child senses their anxiety, and there is an interplay between parent and child that causes some alteration in the standard parent-child relationship.

In the studies I have undertaken in an attempt to understand more fully the psychological effects of chronic illness in children, I have come to realize that these children and their families are much like any other children and any other families. I have observed that if there are any weaknesses in the family situation such as a poor marriage, or personality disturbances among members of the family, the problem of a handicapped child or a child with a chronic illness can cause some breakdown within that family. On the other hand, whatever strengths the family has to begin with are brought into play. Whatever defenses or adaptations are available are mobilized against the illness or handicap that causes the psychological stress. These adaptations and defense mechanisms are what make the families of chronically ill children different.

It is important to recognize how difficult it is for any parent to manage a child with a handicap and how easy it is for an observer to give advice and view the situation without benefit of all the responsibilities entailed and without having been through all the parent's emotional turmoil. All too often the professionals taking care of handicapped children expect them to be exactly like other children except for their illnesses. They do not recognize the special relationship between parent and child and think the parent's feelings are inappropriate. They are inclined to blame the parent for the difficulties they, the professionals, are having in treating the child. Unfortunately, this unkind attitude frequently gets conveyed to the parent and tends to instill feelings of anxiety and inadequacy. What is worse, doctors sometimes give parents advice that is very hard for them to follow because of the nature of their feelings toward their child.

Because chronic illness or a handicap constitutes a stress, an emotionally healthy child is much better able to cope with a disabling situation than a child who has some emotional weakness to begin with. This, like many other situations I have described, emphasizes the importance of providing your child with emotional stability early in life. This early stability will serve him well in coping with whatever stresses occur later on. Whatever the child's resources, the parent's role is to help him cope with the stresses of life.

Chapter XI

❀❀❀❀❀❀❀❀❀❀❀❀❀

Siblings

*When should I tell my child I
am going to have a baby?*

I think it's only fair to tell your child about a new baby as
soon as your pregnancy is discussed with any other members
of your family. Tell your child in the same way you tell him
about other important family concerns. For some strange reason many parents feel that it is wrong to say anything until
the new baby is about to be born. There is no sense whatsoever in this approach. In fact, I can think of no better way
to prepare your child for a new brother or sister than to
include him in the situation as soon as it becomes apparent
to others that a new baby is on the way. If you leave your
child out of discussions and hide the fact that you are pregnant (which would obviously have to be deliberately hidden
since everyone else in the family is discussing it), you may
give him the idea that the sibling-to-be is not anticipated
with happiness and joy.

*Will my child want to know
where the baby is coming
from?*

Yes, and he will want to know much more than just where
the baby is coming from, depending, of course, on his age

and whatever you've told him previously. A child usually wants to know where you are getting him, and who helps. On the other hand, some children don't ask any questions and may let the whole matter ride, showing no curiosity. But it has been my experience that youngsters who are apparently unconcerned have in some way been led to believe the whole matter is highly mysterious and should not be discussed.

If your child asks, be sure to tell him the truth. If you tell him anything else, you will have great difficulty explaining why you go to the hospital when you ultimately do. If you lie initially, you will need to continue with other lies. The unhappy situation gets worse.

Will my child want a sibling of the same sex?

Not necessarily, but he may have some idea of which sex he wants and quite angry if he doesn't get it. Some children want siblings of the opposite sex, particularly if they are at the age to be curious about anatomical differences. Obviously their interest may be transitory. Alternatively, your child may have an interest in a sibling of the same sex in hopes of an amiable playmate and good companion. I think you should help your child realize that it is perfectly understandable to have a specific wish but that no one and specifically neither parent can control what happens. If your child does not recognize this and his wish is not fulfilled, he may think you deliberately denied him his choice.

Some parents tell a child that they feel it is not very important whether the baby is a boy or a girl. They say the important thing is that the child "should love" whatever comes along. This pronouncement reflects a moralistic attitude that your child will have difficulty accepting. At the same time it reflects an adult attitude that ignores your child's feelings. After all, the child thinks, how can you know you will love this creature that hasn't even been seen and is unknown to everyone? If you insist that your child should love this unknown object, you could instill a feeling of guilt if your child has, as he will have, attitudes of competitiveness, jealousy, or hostility, when he thinks of something intruding into your currently "stable" family.

What do I tell my child if I have a miscarriage or if the baby dies?

Children do not have the same feelings about a miscarriage or stillbirth that an adult has. I do not mean that they have less feeling, just that their ideas are different. When telling your child about a miscarriage, explain it to him so he can understand. For example, tell him that a baby was expected, but that something went wrong; tell him that the baby didn't begin to grow in quite the right way, so that the baby you all anticipated won't ever be born. Naturally, if your child has some understanding of reproduction, miscarriage or stillbirth will be easier to explain. You could use the analogy of planting a seed and not having it grow properly.

If a baby is born and dies, again tell your child the truth. Just what you say depends to a large extent upon his age. In general, you should tell your child that the baby was born but something was wrong with it, and it was not able to live. At the same time, don't hesitate to express grief and disappointment but explain that nothing could have been done to make the baby live. Perhaps the most crucial factor to consider at this time is the possibility that your child had some unexpressed wishes that the baby would not be born or that it would die. Your child may feel that his wish came true. If this is the case, your child may experience a great feeling of guilt. He may also have feelings of tremendous power and omnipotence. After all, if he wishes something and it comes true, he'd better be careful what he wishes the next time. This is why you must make it clear to your child that the miscarriage, death, or stillbirth was something that nobody could do anything about. Incidentally, your child will probably have other questions such as "Where is the baby now?" "What will they do with him?" and "Will we have another one?" You should answer these questions as directly and honestly as you possibly can. For example, you could appropriately say that it is too early to want another baby because of your sadness, but that perhaps sometime in the future you may want to have another one.

What will my child feel when I begin labor and go to the hospital?

Generally speaking, your child feels somewhat abandoned and unhappy when his mother goes off to the hospital to have a baby. Often he wonders why his mother wants to have a new baby. His thoughts include: Is there anything wrong with me? Am I not good enough? Will she still love me when she comes home? Does she still remember me? What are they doing to her? Will the doctor hurt her taking the baby out of her? Will she be loving the baby, hugging and kissing him and forgetting all about me? Feelings of abandonment and unworthiness may occur. Clearly, this is a very traumatic time in your child's life. While no really scientific studies have been done, most clinicians dealing with disturbed behavior in children have at some time related the birth of a sibling (the traumatic event) to behavior disorders that developed later.

To make the situation even worse, when the new baby is actually born, everyone is happy and excited. They discuss the new baby, whom he resembles, how healthy he is, what his name will be. With all the festivities, happiness, and joy, and with everyone saying, "Aren't you happy that you have a new baby brother?" your child becomes acutely aware of being left out. He does not feel part of the activity revolving around the new member of the family, whom he neither knows nor even particularly wants. Since it is impossible for you to dampen the enthusiasm over the new baby (and you wouldn't want to, anyway), the best thing you can do to help your older child cope with the new sibling is to tell him early and quite openly everything that will happen, both pleasant and unpleasant.

In preparing my own child for the birth of a new sibling, I emphasized the many negative aspects. I warned him that my wife and I would not have as much time to spend with him alone, that we would no longer have the peace and quiet we were used to, that we would have screams and cries during the night and in the midst of conversation, and that we might have to call upon him to help in caring for this new intruder. I think I may have been inclined to overdo it, for my son looked somewhat frightened from time to time. But apparently not. Two weeks after the baby came home from the hospital he said, one evening at dinner, "Dad, it wasn't half as bad as you said it was going to be."

*How will my child feel when
the baby first comes home?*

Having a new baby come home from the hospital is a momentous occasion in your youngster's life. In some ways it is an irreversible tragedy. After all, your older child now has to contend with a new individual who is a total stranger, who requires all kinds of delicate handling, who receives endless affection, and who is admired by all visitors. And not only do they admire the baby, they shower him with gifts. To top it all off, most people ask, "Don't you like your new baby brother [or sister]?" Absolutely no one seems concerned about his innermost feelings, which are ambivalent at best.

I don't mean to paint too negative a picture, because some children are eager and interested to see their new baby brother or sister, particularly little girls, who anticipate the role of mother surrogate. Little girls who like playing with dolls and who may be as much as five or six years older than the new baby often enjoy an infant in the house.

What can I do to minimize my child's resentment?

The best way is to prepare your child fairly early in your pregnancy for the advent of his new sibling. It also helps if you handle the "introductions" between your children properly. Don't make the common mistake of constantly telling your older child to keep away from the fragile baby. If you do, it should not surprise you that a feeling of resentment ensues. Include the older child in what is going on, and let him help in caring for the baby.

Incidentally, society should help with this problem by implementing a totally new procedure in hospitals. Arrangements should be made to allow your child to come to the hospital, visit his mother, and see his new sibling as soon after the baby is born as the mother is able to smile, express warmth, and respond to a visitor. Bringing your child into the situation at this early time, provided the mother has not had complications, can have nothing but positive results. Among other things, it gives your child a chance to see that his mother is all right. You know this, but your child does not. Often a child believes that the doctor has cut his mother open, removed the baby, and left her without help. Many children who have this fantasy have been told that the baby is in Mommy's tummy and that the doctor will take it out. You would be amazed at how many children who visit their mothers shortly after delivery are surprised to find their mothers happy, healthy, and in pleasant surroundings.

Taking your child to the hospital also allows him to be involved in the festivities and happiness accompanying the birth of a new baby. Seeing both his mother and his sister so excited and being part of the excitement will be a very important experience. Being left out can have no advantages whatsoever, might contribute markedly to feelings of hostility, and might increase sibling rivalry. I recommend these early visits strongly for the sake of the child, but I think they are equally important for the mother. I have known many mothers who feel depressed because they miss the children they have left at home and are not allowed to see.

The common objection to having children come into a hospital centers on their carrying germs. This is nonsense. Adult visitors are equally capable of carrying infections. Although it is true that children carry some germs more dangerous to newborns, this danger can be easily dealt with by having the young visitors checked beforehand. In short, I see no reason at all for continuing the inhumane process of keeping children from visiting their mothers in a maternity hospital. All that is required is to alter the existing procedure slightly to eliminate whatever hazards exist, hazards that are emphasized to maintain the separation of mother and child for the convenience of the hospital staff.

Is sibling rivalry normal?

The best way to answer this question is to say that sibling rivalry is common. Because it is common, it is statistically normal. But I prefer to look upon the situation differently. It is true that children close in age and dependent upon adults for certain care are inclined to be competitive for the attention of those adults. On the other hand, just as rivalry occurs at home, it also occurs between children in a classroom, in a play group, or in a camp. For this reason I cannot consider sibling rivalry as being much different from the struggle young children have to achieve recognition and attention from any adult caring for them. My opinion is reinforced because I know of cases where siblings are not jealous of each other. When I have pointed this out to some of my psychoanalytic colleagues, I have been informed that the children are "repressing" the feelings of rivalry. I am afraid I cannot accept this notion since it is not supported by later observations of the same children.

When sibling rivalry develops, it is usually based upon real events in your child's life. For example, if your child has had his needs met throughout life and has been satisfied in his relationships with you and if the birth of a sibling interferes with this relationship, it is understandable that your child will feel rivalry toward his sibling. If, on the other hand, the birth of a sibling does not result in a lessening of love and affection, measured not upon your expressed feeling, but upon the amount of time you spend with your child and other subtle indicators of your feelings, your child need not feel resentful.

It is worth noting again that the intensity of sibling rivalry is very often a direct result of how you have dealt with the birth of a new sibling and the degree to which you have allowed the new baby to interfere with the relationships you have previously established with your older children. The extent of sibling rivalry is also related to the age difference between children. If your child is eighteen months of age when a new sibling is born, obviously he has to share his mother a great deal because an eighteen-month-old child is still extremely dependent upon his mother. But if the age difference is five years, and the older sibling has already established contacts in the outside world, he is less aware of having to share with a new sibling. In my experience, the great amounts of time and interest that a parent must devote to the newborn child will seem less challenging to your older child if he is at least three years old.

Can I do anything to minimize sibling rivalry?

You can recognize that you must try to treat each child as an individual from the very beginning. Often parents will prepare a child for the birth of a sibling by explaining, "When the new baby comes, we won't stop loving you. We will love both you and the baby just as much." The well-meaning parent who adopts this point of view is actually setting the stage for sibling rivalry by making a direct comparison between the older child and the new sibling. Don't make this kind of pronouncement, because while you may be trying to convince your child that your love will be equal, your child may not be getting that message. What concerns him is whether you are telling the truth or not. Your child has no choice but to test your honesty and the credibility of your statement, which means constantly putting you to the test of "equal love." To avoid this trap, start by explaining that all people are different, and no one ever loves two people in the same way. Then you have set the stage for explaining that your responses to the new baby and to the older sibling will be different. After all, how can you treat a baby the same way you do an older child?

Many parents set the stage for sibling rivalry in their attempts to minimize it. A well-meaning friend of mine always asks people to give the same gift to each of his two daughters at Christmas. He is constantly sensitive that his children may discern differences in the presents they receive, the time people spend with them, and their parents' expressions of affection. Because my friend reacts the way he does, his children are much more consciously aware of any differences that happen to occur. I would be inclined to handle each child as an individual, and, if anything, I would encourage friends to give them different gifts. If one child happens to like the gift the other child got more than the one he himself received, I would simply point out to the child that that's the way things are, that life has its frustrations, and that sometimes you may just have to accept disappointment. In short, by minimizing the comparative statements, by minimizing attempts to equate everything, and by emphasizing individuality, you can help your child cope with his feelings of sibling rivalry.

What about twins?

In general, twins are really like all other children. The same principles that apply to other siblings apply to them, though in some ways twins have an easier time than siblings of different ages, simply because a parent can more easily, though erroneously, equate things for them. It is wiser to make every attempt to treat them as individuals, even though they may look alike and may even be confused by other people. If you do regard them as individuals and emphasize their individuality, rivalry between them will be diminished.

As most people know, twins are usually very much aware of which one was born first. In fact, they are much more conscious of the age difference, minute as it is, than other children whose ages are farther apart. The degree to which differences become important to twins is proportional to the amount of emphasis placed upon treating them similarly. Incidentally, treating any child as an individual does not necessarily mean constantly telling him that he is different. It does mean your reacting to each child in a different manner.

*Are there special problems for
an only child?*

Yes. If your child is an only child, he is not going to have to share with his siblings. Consequently, dealing with children his own age will be a less familiar process. Generally speaking, an only child receives considerable attention from both his parents and may very well expect this kind of attention elsewhere in life. I don't mean that all only children will demand and expect undivided attention; I simply mean that the relationships in the family in which an only child lives lend themselves to this development. All you as a parent can do is be aware of the tendency and attempt to counteract it. Let your child play with other children. Encourage group activities, particularly when they involve give and take with other children. Interestingly enough, an only child often longs for a sibling. Children with siblings, on the other hand, often long to be only children. This observation, if anything, suggests that sibling rivalry is not inborn, but is a phenomenon that is largely learned.

Is my oldest child different
from the younger ones?

Your oldest child is different from your other children for very obvious reasons. He has been an only child for at least some part of his life, whereas all your other children have never had that experience. Usually your oldest child has withstood your lack of experience in handling children. Parents worry more with their first child and are extremely careful in handling him. Not surprisingly, their attitude with subsequent children is more casual and may include indifference to some things they worried about before. Since the age of the parents plays some role in how they handle their children, obviously the oldest child has had parents of a younger age. The oldest child is indeed different because of these factors, even if for no others.

Many studies have been done on differences in the personalities of children that may be related to the ordinal position in the family. Studies generally support the idea that the oldest child tends to be more succesful and works harder to solve problems that are encountered. I find I tend to agree, although there are many many exceptions. This information may help you interpret your child's reactions, though there is little you can do about them except accept them.

Does a middle child have spe-
cial problems?

Some doctors identify a "middle-child syndrome." I'm not sure I would agree that such a thing exists. I have never seen it described with any degree of consistency, and I am inclined to believe that no two children in the middle are alike. It is true, however, that a middle child can be caught between an older sibling who received a great deal of parental attention, particularly when he was an only child, and a younger sibling who is currently being cuddled and babied. In this sense, the middle child has had to relinquish some of his share of his parents' attention to a new sibling while recognizing that his older sibling sets the trend which parents admire or reject.

Many middle children seem confused by their position in the family. Others develop personality characteristics that provide them with adequate attention to give them some feeling of self-esteem. In my experience many middle children are more outgoing, sometimes exhibitionistic, and very often clownish. In a sense they have resolved their problem by finding the least common denominator that gives them recognition from both older and younger siblings. They find the level of humor that amuses both the older and younger siblings.

What about the latecomer?

The latecomer, a child born a considerable time after his siblings, sometimes unexpectedly and often unplanned, is usually highly welcome. He is a renaissance for his family. He is greatly indulged by all members of the family, particularly as there is usually little rivalry or jealousy between him and his siblings. The new arrival has many playmates and receives a great deal of stimulation. Often older siblings accept surrogate-parent responsibilities. One of your problems, of course, is that these babies are often overindulged.

Another problem stems from your own parental reaction. Most parents of latecomers, in my experience, enjoy their youngest child. They want him to stay young forever. They tend to keep him dependent. While there is no harm in indulging yourself a bit in this direction, don't overdo it.

Incidentally, you ought to know that a pregnant mother can be embarrassing to older children. Teenagers are the most inclined to feel this way. They are quite conscious of sex, and their mother's pregnancy is an obvious hallmark of a sexual activity they may be reluctant to acknowledge. If they themselves are hesitant to see the sex in the situation, you can be sure their adolescent friends will bring it to their attention.

*Should I treat an adopted child
any differently from a natural-
born child?*

If you have adopted a newborn infant, which is the common practice, I recommend that you treat him just like a natural-born child. You may find it somewhat difficult to get used to the child, but, in fact, your adaptation is not much different from the experience of natural parents at the time their child is born in a hospital.

It is absolutely natural for your child, adopted or not, to look in the mirror and wonder which parent he looks like or if he looks like either. Sometimes your natural-born has the fantasy that maybe he was adopted and no one has told him. Many children go through many months of anguish guessing at the truth, asking their parents over and over again, never seeming to accept reassurance that they were not adopted. In this sense, adopted children are no different from natural-born children, since they have all had the experience, at least in fantasy, of having been adopted.

*Are there problems if I adopt a
child and then have one of my
own?*

That's a little different. If one child has been adopted, he has probably been told that his natural parents were unable to care for him, that his adoptive parents, unable to have a child, wanted one so badly that they asked for him. This explanation is supposed to give the adopted child a feeling that he is not only wanted but even more appreciated than a natural child. If you then have a natural child, it is just possible that your older adopted child may feel that you no longer want him because you prefer your own natural child. This is a very delicate matter that is difficult to handle.

Perhaps the only way you can deal with the situation is by expressing real, sincere warmth and affection for all your children. Offering more love and affection to your adopted child in an attempt to compensate for the possibility that he may feel unloved will only make him more suspicious. You might have avoided the whole situation simply by not telling your child that you adopted him because you couldn't have children of your own. Just emphasize that you wanted children very badly, whether you had them yourself or took an infant whose parents were unable to care for him. With this approach you can get across the idea that children themselves are more important to you than where they come from.

Will I have problems if I adopt a child after I have had children of my own?

A child who has been adopted and is aware that his other siblings are all natural children may feel left out. Dealing with this problem requires openness on your part. You must help the adopted child understand how much you wanted him and how important he is to you. Of course, if you have treated each of your natural children as individuals, and if you treat him as another individual, he will be less inclined to feel different from the others. Naturally, if there is plenty of love and affection to go around, there will be less jealousy and rivalry for what's available.

One of the hazards that your adopted child may encounter is the cruelty children sometimes show to each other. For example, if his siblings become angry with him, it is perfectly possible that they will say, "Your real mother didn't even want you, and we had to take you because of that." Remarks like this are not uncommon among children when they are angry. Needless to say, this kind of remark could be very upsetting to your adopted child. If a situation like this ever arises, deal with it openly, immediately, and directly by making it very clear to the adopted child and his angry siblings that he was taken into the family because you wanted him and loved him.

Is it to my child's advantage to have siblings?

It is hard for me to answer this question unequivocally. But I am inclined to think that it is to your child's advantage to have siblings. Siblings create certain stresses which, if overcome successfully, help give your child resources that can be adapted to deal with other situations later on in life, particularly those involving people his own age. If your child has siblings, he learns how to share, how to come face to face with his own greed and jealousy, and how to accept his own individuality, particularly if you emphasize his individuality when you are helping him share within the family. In addition, siblings are companions for each other, and in spite of the hostilities that sometimes arise, they are often quick to come to each other's aid when an outside aggressor threatens.

If your child has siblings, he also sees you deal with different children in different ways. This experience not only helps him establish a feeling of individuality, but helps him understand children better. This knowledge will be valuable to him when he becomes a parent. He learns not only by having siblings, but by watching his parents handling his siblings.

Family gatherings can be happy events and are often the source of pleasant memories for many people. They remember holidays, anniversaries, and other festive occasions with great nostalgia. Often people try to recreate these experiences when they themselves get married and have children. Obviously, a family gathering including several siblings is enriched. Moreover, when the siblings get married and have children, the children will have cousins and aunts and uncles, some of whom they will like, others of whom they may not. In either case, the child is part of a complete family.

Chapter XII

Your Child's Education

When should I start educating
my child?
Experiments have shown quite clearly that newborn infants are capable of learning, learning that is not terribly complex, but still learning. The newborn baby is quite capable of recording experiences, particularly since he is highly sensitive to environmental conditions. For example, a baby will quickly learn to wiggle his foot if it is connected to a mobile that moves when he wiggles. If you then connect it to his other foot you will see him move that one also. A vast body of knowledge is rapidly accumulating which shows that these early experiences have a rather profound impact on later behavior. I believe you can and should educate your child from the time of birth onward. At first, this means providing an environment for your newborn that includes varied sensory stimulation. We know that if you stimulate your baby in this way it will increase his capacity for learning.

In the early education of your child, toys play a very important role. In early infancy they provide sensory stimulation. As your child grows and begins to want to play with objects and understand more about how the world functions, he will find lifting things, dropping things, feeling things, and moving things about valuable learning experiences. During his second year, having toys that react when he does something to them not only fascinates him but gives him some idea that he can change the external environment. If toys are given to your child as objects to satisfy his curiosity and his interest in exploring the environment, your child can't have too many toys. Many educational toys put out by toy manufacturers are expensive, complicated, and fascinating to children. However, many household items, particularly kitchen utensils, have about the same interest for children. All toys, including everyday objects, are extremely beneficial to your child's continued intellectual growth. But it is of the utmost importance that you do not use toys as rewards for good behavior or allow them to represent parental love.

Before your child understands language, play is essential to learning. Later, when your child does begin to understand language, learning by talking as well as playing begins. Your child starts to ask questions and get answers. Any child whose questions have been answered develops a seemingly insatiable desire to ask more questions and get more answers. In fact, children pass through stages when they seem to ask questions simply for the sake of asking the question. At least, it appears that way to the poor parent who has to answer the same question over and over again. The child seems delighted that he can cause his parent to say things that were said before. You sometimes get the impression that the onslaught of questions from a three-year-old serves to keep you on your toes, ready to explain more about the world.

Some parents with the best intentions force learning on a young child. They put pictures with words in big letters all over the house to teach their child to recognize these words. As far as I'm concerned, the parent who pushes learning in this way has missed the boat. He is not helping his child with the learning processes that are appropriate, and he may very well foul up a good parent-child relationship by acting as a teacher in a formal manner. Parents who force children to learn are simply satisfying their own need to show how smart their children are. All they will accomplish is to deface the walls.

When is my child ready for school?

Most children are ready to begin school around the age of three. By then most children are weaned, toilet trained, and show enough independence to be able to spend prolonged periods of time away from their mothers. Putting your child into a formal school situation any earlier is not advisable. A younger child is not really ready to engage in group activities with other children, since most children under the age of three engage in what is described as "parallel play." In other words, they play alongside each other, but do not interact in any meaningful way. In fact, there is a good chance that the children will merely frustrate each other, which makes a child belligerent, defensive, and perhaps less receptive to the pleasures of playing with other children in the future.

Putting your child in school before the appropriate time also separates him from his mother when contact with his mother may still be important for his growing sense of self-confidence. Your child should not be pushed like this, since the proper way to promote healthy emotional development is to satisfy your child's early emotional needs, not frustrate them. If your child has had a satisfying infancy and has succeeded in mastering weaning and toilet training, and if your child's questions about the world have been answered, he will be ready and will want to go to school without coaxing from you.

Will play groups prepare my child for school?

For the moment, let us define a play group as a group of children more or less formally organized for supervision by an adult while they play. Learning, formal or informal, is not the purpose. A play group can help your child cope with separation from his mother if he masters the anxiety he will feel at first. A play group can give your child an opportunity for contact with other children. It can give him a chance to play with new toys. In short, your child can learn something from a play group, but I think that for the most part, play groups are intended to be baby-sitters for parents who want to do something away from their children. The supposed educational importance is sheer rationalization; play groups are not as important for your child's growth and development as they have been made to seem.

As far as I am concerned, freeing mothers is a perfect reason for organizing play groups. They need not be turned into an "important learning experience for your child." Many parents basically do not enjoy playing with their children or engaging them in activities that fulfill some developmental need. These parents often feel guilty and carry out their "obligations" simply to assuage their guilt. Other mothers seem to engage in some activity *alongside* their children but never engage in an activity *with* them. Many mothers spend a lot of time with their children, but do it in this sort of "adjacent" way. They are perfectly good mothers, who don't seem to have any deep-rooted fascination for simple play with young children. My experience tells me that their children would probably be better off in a play group than at home with a mother who either resents doing what she feels she should do or who, by sidestepping any play activities with her child, deprives him of the opportunity to play. Whether you send your child to a play group or keep him at home should depend to a large extent upon which environment is more stimulating for your child.

What should I tell my child
about going to school?

Most children are eager to begin school. This is equally true for the child who will attend nursery school around the age of three and for the child who attends kindergarten at five. Your child probably knows an older child who attends school and wants to do the same. Your job is not to induce interest, but to reduce anxiety.

When you prepare your child for school, stick to the concrete facts about what he will be doing there. If you explain the anticipated experience in terms of when he will go, what he will do there, and when you will pick him up, he will have a clearer view of the whole situation than if you tell him how wonderful school is and how much fun he will have there and what nice little children he will meet. These latter statements are interpretive comments, not literal descriptions of what he will encounter. If you do not tell him the literal facts, he will make them up, arriving at a concept totally different from reality. For example, one child I know, having been told that school would be a great deal of fun, was terribly disappointed after his first day because he encountered numerous crying youngsters who were asking for their mothers rather than playing with this child who anticipated "great fun." Because of the contrast between what he was told and what he actually found, it was hard to convince him that things would begin to get better as time went on. As far as he was concerned, he had been misled and had no reason to believe that school would be any different the second day.

Don't forget to tell your child that he will be staying in school alone with the teacher and the other children and that you will return to pick him up later. You might also let him know that at first he may be unhappy and lonely, but that eventually he will get used to school. At the same time, explain that some children may even cry when their mommies leave. Be sure to tell him about all the things that might occur so that he will be prepared, should these events actually occur. If you outline a completely rosy picture and something disquieting happens, his disappointment may overwhelm him and so preoccupy him that he cannot play with other children, talk with his teacher, or absorb the subject that is being taught. Incidentally, it can be very helpful if the teacher visits your child in his own home some time before school begins.

How will my child react to starting school?

Although children are generally delighted at the idea of going to school, they often find the first day or two disconcerting. Even if you thoroughly prepare your child for the experience of starting school, it still represents a milestone in your child's life because it involves detaching himself from his mother and entering a new environment with many uncertainties and a host of new people. For this reason, many schools encourage parents to spend the first day with their children and may even encourage them to stay a while each day thereafter until the child adjusts to school.

Generally, if going to school is a natural continuation of a normal learning process begun much earlier in your child's life, and if the school is geared to soothing some of the anxieties your child may encounter, the experience of going to school can be a happy one. As a great challenge successfully met, it adds to your child's self-esteem. That is why so many children "bloom" at school.

Why, then, do some children react negatively to going to school?

In my experience a child who does not want to go to school is often anxious about being away from his mother. Perhaps his anxiety is warranted, particularly if he views going to school as being "kicked out of the house." Sometimes, when there are younger siblings at home, a child may feel that he is being deprived of maternal attention, particularly as his siblings may be getting increased amounts of his mother's affection. He feels his own position is threatened. Some children will react negatively if they find the teacher scary and unresponsive to their needs. Sometimes other children in the class who bully or terrorize cause or enhance a negative attitude. Sometimes a child simply does not, with justification, like what the teacher makes him do.

A child may dislike school if there are tensions in his family, particularly marital discord. The child's fears and uncertainties seem to increase at school when he is away from his home. Because the situation at home is unstable, the child feels insecure and needs constantly to reassure himself that both his parents are still there. When he seems preoccupied and inattentive to his work, he is probably ruminating about the situation at home. The uncertainty about what he will find when he gets home increases his anxiety.

What should I do when my
child reacts negatively to his
initial school experience?

It is important that you stay in school with your child if this happens. Some children simply need a longer period of time to adjust to school and seem less ready to be separated from a parent who they know provides security. Some children react this way because they have had numerous separation experiences, some of them frightening. If you accompany your child long enough to establish the idea that school is a friendly place, he will develop confidence and learn that the teacher will be there to comfort him and protect him if need be.

Sometimes your child's negative reaction is caused by your preparation. If an overprotective parent repeatedly warns his child of numerous hazards that may occur and emphasizes the disastrous consequences, his child will be less inclined to feel comfortable away from the parent. Sometimes a parent is reluctant to send a child off to school and may unconsciously communicate his own anxiety to the child.

Sure enough, the child becomes reluctant about remaining in school. For all these problems the cure is the same: Stay with your child.

Unfortunately, some schools allow a child to decide when his parent may leave him alone in school. I feel this decision should not be left solely to the child. A child's readiness to let his parent go should be determined by the adults involved rather than the child. Naturally they should take into consideration the child's feelings. Many children, when given the power to make this decision, continue to be anxious. The reason is that no child still dependent on parents to protect him can help being anxious if he is expected to take responsibility for leaving these same parents. A responsibility like that is a parent's.

What should I do about my child who, after a period of adjustment, decides he doesn't want to attend school any longer?

This reaction is very common. When it happens, most parents react as if the child is at fault. They feel he is being unduly dependent on his parents. I think it is much more sensible to ask the school what has been going on before blaming your child. Often your child has encountered a specific problem, perhaps a particular child who bullies him or a frightening occurrence he is unwilling to discuss. Let me remind you that the teacher may be the cause of your child's resistance. If your child is reacting to unpleasantness, you should take action to solve his problem. Follow through and help your child see that you have come to his assistance and attempted to stop the cause of his fear.

Another common reason for your child's reluctance to attend school after his initial adjustment may be that he is unable to perform at the level that is expected of him. His inability can lead to a sense of failure and make him wish to flee from this unpleasant feeling. Exuberant parents, who push a child without considering his capacity to cope, often cause the problem. At the same time, there are parents who do the opposite. They tend to hold onto a child and keep him dependent. Naturally, their children would rather be at home than at school.

Whatever the cause, I feel strongly that you should *not* allow your child to remain home from school, even if his reluctance to go is great. At the first sign of resistance, when your child says, "I have a stomach ache and feel like I may throw up if I go to school," get in touch with the school. If your child knows you are trying to solve his problem while you are insisting that he attend school, you will be teaching him two of life's important lessons. The first is that when problems occur, they need to be dealt with. The second is that while dealing with problems, a person often has to do something even if he doesn't want to. If your child is allowed to stay home, it becomes increasingly difficult to get him back to school. In addition, you are supporting a pattern of avoiding problems rather than teaching the process of facing them.

*What do I do if my child feigns
physical illness?*

Children often complain of physical illness to avoid school, a particularly perplexing problem, because no parent wants to send a sick child off to school. I think it is not only reasonable but helpful to your child if you set certain ground rules about when he can stay home because of physical complaints. I would recommend a doctor's agreement as one criterion. The other criterion I would recommend, if your child complains often and if the complaints are vague and mild, is an elevated temperature. Allowing your child to stay at home just because he has a minor physical complaint supports the use of physical illness as a means of avoiding stress. Carried to extremes, your child might become a hypochondriac who relies on physical-distress symptoms to avoid responsibility.

Needless to say, the possibility always exists that you will send your child off to school in spite of his complaints only to find that he did in fact have a real illness. While no parent wants to make this mistake, it is better to take some chance than to allow your child to remain at home whenever he has minor complaints. When you send a complaining child off to school, he may react as if you don't believe him. I think you have to make it clear that it's not as much a matter of disbelief as the fact that his physical complaints are not so severe that they warrant his staying home from school. At the same time, you might point out that people often have to do things in spite of their aches and pains. If you are an anxious parent concerned about taking this approach, you might be reassured by calling the school to check on your child's health sometime in the course of the day.

What should I do if my child
won't tell me about school?

While some children are eager to talk about their school experiences, for the most part, children frequently do not like to go into detailed descriptions of what took place in school. School is a part of their private life. I think you should respect your child's reluctance to tell you about school. But it is equally important for you to show continued interest in what goes on, how he is doing, and in whether he is having any problems. Forcing your child to talk about school or acting impatient when your child hesitates to discuss it will usually make him feel you are infringing on his privacy and snooping into his life. The more you pressure your child, the more likely he will continue to balk. It has been my experience that getting information about school from boys between the ages of seven and twelve is like pulling teeth.

*Should I participate in school
activities?*

I don't consider it essential for you to participate in school activities, but I think that most children get a secret satisfaction in knowing that their parents consider school sufficiently important to be interested. Don't go to class with your child, but do go to parents' day and teachers' conferences. Your participation gives your child the feeling that there is a free flow of information between you and his teacher. Your child will have more respect for his teachers and the school if you consider the school important. I have found that children whose parents participate in school activities learn a kind of communal spirit and develop a sense of responsibility about community matters.

Any child regards school as if it were a little bit like his own family and his own family a little bit like school. Having a teacher to dinner is generally a special occasion for a child that eases communication between your child and his teacher. After all, if your child's teacher knows a little about your home and your family, your child feels that his teacher is a little more involved in his life.

I think the idea of inviting a teacher to dinner should be discussed with your child in advance, and the invitation should be issued only if your child agrees. On such an occasion your child should be given the chance to assume some responsibilities for the dinner itself and the opportunity to show off a little bit for his teacher. Passing the main platter or clearing the table by himself is an independent task for your child and tells the teacher the child feels he is a participating member of a family and capable of assuming a significant role. Obviously, you should not use an occasion like this to embarrass your child or to point out his shortcomings. Nor is this the time to discuss any of his school problems.

Why do some children dislike homework?

Many children dislike doing homework, some more than others. A child's approach depends to a large extent on the amount of homework he gets and whether or not the homework is intellectually stimulating. Unfortunately, parents often contribute to a child's dislike for homework. For example, a parent may insist that his child do all his homework immediately following school before he can engage in any other activities that are fun. By so doing the parent makes the homework an obstacle to pleasure. The child quite naturally resents the dislocation.

Teachers, too, may be responsible. A teacher who assigns subjects that are boring or repetitive simply to give a pupil some "busy work" can cause a child to dislike his homework. Worse, some teachers treat homework as if it were a form of punishment. For example, a teacher will give no homework to children who have gotten good grades while assigning homework to others who have done poorly or who have misbehaved. This practice immediately creates a non-educational purpose for homework, and homework becomes tantamount to punishment. If this happens, any child will logically dislike homework. If a teacher grades homework so severely that a child is panicked by the possibility of making errors, then anxiety and fear interfere with his doing homework. Consider all the facts associated with your child's reluctance to do homework if and when this problem arises.

More often than not, you will find the homework assignment is realistic. Even so, your child may not want to do it. If so, acknowledge your child's feelings, agree that he may not like to do homework, but tell him he must do it anyway.

*How can I get my child to like
doing homework?*

It may be asking too much to expect your child to like doing homework, but I think you can get him to accept it. Assist your child as much as you can, but without doing the homework for him. Some parents find it easier when pressed by a child who is anxious to get homework done to do it for him. This serves no purpose and does not really assist your child. One of the best ideas is to help your child establish a routine for doing homework, preferably one that involves no friction with you and that is compatible with his other after-school activities, though I think you should expect your child to do his homework at a reasonable hour. It helps to provide a quiet and comfortable environment for him to work in.

Your attitude about your child's homework will have the greatest influence on his acceptance or rejection of homework as a meaningful activity. If you treat homework as an unpleasant task and take a punitive attitude about doing it, you convey the idea that homework is not something to be liked, but something to be done. On the other hand, if you help your child with homework in the right way, it can be made to be fascinating, stimulating, even fun. If this is the case, your child will enjoy homework and feel satisfied when it's complete.

*How do I know whether my
child is adjusted to school?*

Positive adjustment to school is evident by a child's eagerness to attend school, his willingness to do homework even if he doesn't like it, making friends through school and continuing his relationship with them, and by some interest in the learning process itself. Obviously, good school reports are meaningful, but do not accept a good school report as the only criterion for a happy school adjustment. Some children will produce good reports in school simply because they fear punishment or are anxious about failure.

What are the symptoms of a
poor school adjustment?

Usually, a child who has made a poor school adjustment will begin to be reluctant to attend school. While reluctance is generally a reliable indicator, some children seem to enjoy school in spite of the fact that they are not adjusting. Although they are learning practically nothing, their emotional needs are being adequately satisfied. Poor grades; behavioral disturbances, such as increased irritability, increased anxiety, and fearfulness; and mild habit disturbances, such as nail-biting, occasional bed-wetting, and stammering or stuttering, may represent pressures in adjusting to school. They show that a child is having difficulty coping and needs assistance. Whenever you notice any signs of behavior disturbance or difficulty with the learning process itself, you should consider whether your child is adjusting to school. If the problem persists, if other problems of the type I have mentioned crop up, too, you should consult the school and find out what is happening.

Sometimes your child may have a learning disability associated with some minor neurological dysfunction or with some constitutional factor such as a glandular disturbance. Then your child's problem is not primarily emotional. Many of these physiological problems appear to be emotional disturbances. In reality they are caused by a learning disability that forces your child to act disturbed when he cannot cope with a conventional learning situation. A neurological problem usually begins in the first or second grade. Common symptoms are difficulty in learning to read, poor handwriting, hyperactivity, and short attention span. Often there are accompanying emotional problems that are secondary to a learning disability.

Whenever any evidence of a poor school adjustment exists, I think you must deal with the problem. A child who is pushed from grade to grade but whose adjustment problems have not been diagnosed or dealt with, often becomes enmeshed in problems that seem to multiply. They rapidly become so insurmountable that only massive remedial help can untangle the mess. School years are a critical stage in your child's development. Once they have gone, there is no opportunity to go back and correct the problems that developed then. Generally, school problems that are properly diagnosed can be dealt with rationally, and an educational situation appropriate for your child can be found. Thus, if you suspect, even barely suspect, that your child has a problem, seek assistance from a child psychologist or child psychiatrist who can help diagnose the problem and recommend treatment.

While many schools have staff available to help with these problems, it has been my experience that it is best to bring your child's problems to the attention of your pediatrician and get his help in finding the appropriate professional. Since your pediatrician is the primary medical professional in your child's life, I think it is of the utmost importance that he be aware of all aspects of your child's physical, emotional, and intellectual life.

I want to make one further point that is too often overlooked. Your child's poor school adjustment may result from something that is wrong with the school and not with your child. Parents often, and without evidence, consider their child at fault when any adjustment problem occurs. However, I have seen numerous cases where a school was unable to recognize the needs of the child and was not able to adjust school routines to the individual capabilities of the child. Obviously, poor adjustment must result. Thus, a poorly motivated child may not necessarily be "stupid" or emotionally disturbed. His classroom situation may induce little motivation, or perhaps the learning atmosphere is frightening and threatening because the teacher is too strict. On occasion a child who does poorly may very well be an extremely bright child who is bored by a class that lacks stimulation. In any case, the point I am trying to make is that you consider the possibility that the school is unable to meet your child's special intellectual needs. If you do investigate this possibility, as you should, look into it without letting your child know that you are querying the capacity of the school. If your child senses that you are questioning his teachers' authority or their "stature," he will invariably lose respect for school authorities and may even stop obeying them.

Chapter XIII

Disobedience, Rebellion, and Defiance

Is disobedience normal in the growing child?

Yes. Disobedience occurs to some degree at all stages in your child's development. However, disobedience is meaningless to him until he begins to realize that you have an annoyed or angry reaction when he disregards your wishes. Then your child begins to know what you want and what you do not want. Once he realizes that you expect him to do certain things, he'll have begun to establish controls and limits. And once expected standards of behavior are established, you have set the stage for your child to challenge you. In fact, you can be sure that you will be challenged regularly.

Be pleased that your child does challenge you. One of the major tasks of childhood is to find the structure and meaning of life, which one learns to a large extent by finding out about rules, regulations, and how things happen. As your child gets older, his behavior becomes more complex and varied, and he begins to test you to discover the finer distinctions of your discipline. Your child is not necessarily deliberately trying to make your life miserable; he is simply testing your limits or, really, testing new hypotheses about your reactions to what he does. This kind of disobedience can be

169

considered normal. You do not need to be greatly concerned unless your child is constantly disobedient. If he seems to like making you writhe and if each time you express a wish he disobeys you, then you might begin to be wary.

Should I be concerned, then, if my child always obeys?

If a child always obeys the wishes of his parents, that child has probably been exposed to extremely harsh discipline, including severe punishment. All his individuality has been—sometimes quite literally—beaten out of him. A totally obedient child has usually given up. He shows little interest in expressing himself. His satisfaction comes from following through on the wishes of others. Often such a child is unable to carry out any task unless it is clearly requested and outlined by others. He is subservient. A child who is totally obedient in this way often grows up to be a passive individual who lacks drive, imagination, and initiative.

Incidentally, in the normal school setting, children who always obey are generally highly regarded by their teachers. They are held up as examples. They are extremely polite, courteous, and well liked by adults. They are often referred to as "little ladies" and "little gentlemen." While this behavior may please an adult and is generally encouraged by the adult's reaction, children like this get little satisfaction from childhood. They are often teased by their friends. Sometimes they are overtly rejected. Since their only hope for any kind of adjustment lies in pleasing adults, they are soon unable to express any individuality. This passivity continues in later life.

What does it mean if my child constantly misbehaves?

The child who constantly misbehaves generally has not established internal mechanisms of control over his own behavior. That is, he has not established in his own conscience a set of standards that tell him what is acceptable behavior. The absence of a conscience to self-regulate behavior can have several causes. Often a child who constantly misbehaves is one who has not learned to put off immediate gratification. He cannot delay instant pleasure for later, greater pleasure that can be obtained in a socially acceptable manner. Often these children have grown up in an environment that has not provided them with enough satisfactions at any time to enable them to learn to control their impulses for the reward of some greater, delayed gratification. You see, in order to be able to stand frustration, your child must learn that there is some satisfaction in doing so. He must have been rewarded later for previous self-denial. He must have to overcome the discomfort involved in dealing with obstacles to goals for the satisfaction of achieving those goals. Obviously, if your child has never been rewarded at all, he cannot have learned to delay his gratification.

Constant misbehavior may have another cause. The disobedient child may have happened to have a series of experiences that encouraged his misbehavior. For example, a child might get the label of troublemaker simply because his teacher found it difficult to deal with him. As you might expect, that child may find it easier to continue engaging in "misbehavior" that will conform with his teacher's expectations because it will be more difficult to reverse the teacher's opinion. Thus, he continues to misbehave.

Sometimes constant misbehavior is caused when a child is constantly in situations where the result of every available action is equally impossible. He is punished if he does it one way, and he is punished if he does it the other way. If this happens enough, he learns only that he had better take what he can get now, because there is nothing tomorrow.

I have known numerous children who are basically frightened, who crave affection and acceptance, and who more or less constantly misbehave. Each of these children has grown up in an environment that has offered him little for conforming to any social standards. Some of them have never been rewarded for showing socially acceptable behavior. In fact, many of these children have done better getting what they can as soon as they can rather than putting down their impulses for some future reward. They are regarded as troublemakers and have established at least in that way some role which means something to other people.

When I investigate further, I often find that these children come from homes where their parents are preoccupied with their own problems or for various reasons pay very little attention to their children. They almost have to be forced to notice their children and do so only when their children are in trouble or have some very substantial problem. Nor surprisingly, the children learn rather quickly that they can get their parents' attention if they manage to get into difficulty or deliberately create problems. Their need for parental recognition and for parental discipline shows up when they use negative attention to satisfy their needs. These "disobedient" children have been taught that negative attention is better than being ignored.

*Why would my child want this
kind of attention?*

The chances are that he is not recognized when he is good. No child wants negative attention if positive recognition is forthcoming. There is no inherent desire to behave badly. This is a learned phenomenon, based upon your reactions to your child. If you offer no positive satisfactions or positive attention and only attend to your child's needs when he is misbehaving, you are, in a sense, encouraging this rather unpleasant means for getting your attention.

*What should I do if my child is
constantly   disobedient?*

To begin with, look for the reasons behind his misbehavior. You must identify the problem before you can solve it. No child is continually disobedient without good reason. As I have said, the likelihood is that your child is no longer receiving any positive attention or acceptance from the significant adults in his life. Nor is he receiving any rewards for socially acceptable behavior. His life is built around restrictions, punishment, deprivations. Youngsters with severe problems of disobedience, rebellion, and defiance usually have parents who are too busy to devote time to them or to be interested in their growth and development when they as parents are most needed. Over and over I hear of fathers who do not seem to have time for their sons and who never seem satisfied with their accomplishments. Sometimes it's a mother who wants perfection and who not only disregards her child's belongings and privacy but takes away his only pleasures and satisfactions as punishments for not meeting her demands.

I have often been called into consultations involving a problem child who is invariably disobedient. All too often he does not seem to care; he is unmotivated and doing poorly in school. He can be intelligent and capable, but no matter what restrictions are placed upon him, he does not seem to take an interest in things. The child may seem disinterested in his belongings, as well as in his schoolwork. Sometimes the disobedient behavior involves attacking younger siblings, and when this occurs, parents generally defend the younger sibling, thereby increasing the older child's feelings of persecution. No matter how many privileges are taken away, no matter how many pleasures are restricted, nothing seems to straighten out these children—at least, according to their parents.

In my opinion, there is no mystery about why a child treated like this does not seem to care, is unmotivated, and constantly misbehaves. No matter what this child does right, no matter how well he performs, he remains unacknowledged. There is no satisfaction for him in behaving acceptably, nor does anyone seem to care about his feelings.

Ultimately, he develops a protective shield and could not care less about the feelings of others.

If you have a child who is constantly disobedient, when you have identified his problems, try to dilute the cause of his misbehavior. See that there are some satisfactions and pleasures in his relationship with you. By emphasizing his good points and proper behavior, you can reinstitute the concept of discipline, together with a feeling of protection. You can teach your child that the people who set the rules do not focus only on deprivation and do offer protection and support. If you fail, your child may become vulnerable to the values of others, who just may be bad influences but who nevertheless may be more satisfying companions than his parents.

Then just what does my child want of me?

Your child needs to experience satisfactions in his relationship with you as well as feel the restraints your expectations place upon him. If either the sense of restraint or the sense of satisfaction is lacking, a problem will ensue. An overbearing parent who offers little or no satisfaction will drive his child away from the home. On the other hand, studies have shown over and over again that children brought up in a family without a strong authority figure have a tendency to be delinquent during adolescence. A parent who is absent, is weak in setting standards, or is inconsistent, may inadvertently force his child to seek standards of behavior from someone else—often the child's friends. They too may be having similar problems, and all of them may be alienated from the values and standards of the adult world. This alienation may lead these youngsters to be self-destructive, since they have little wisdom based on past experience. In a sense, they are engaging in a behavioral ritual that gives them all the feeling that they belong and that each cares for the other—a feeling that none of them had in his own family.

Apart from this, your child would like to feel that you know he is a separate individual in his own right and that you recognize his differences. I think he wants you to assist him in using his own resources and to recognize and be proud of his accomplishments. Your support will give him the impetus to carry on and engage in more and more independent activity. If you treat him as if he were going to fail, or if he feels he may encounter overwhelming problems without your constant surveillance and support, you will inhibit his spontaneity and discourage him from using his own best capabilities.

In my opinion, deeply felt, there is no such thing as "giving your child too much of the best of everything," if you are truly giving of yourself. Children can be very demanding during the time when standards of behavior are normally learned and self-incorporated from an authority figure within the family who is both respected and loved. A good parent who responds to his child's demands returns the child's feelings—that is, the feelings of love and respect. Only mutual and reciprocal love and respect (the two faces of discipline) fully supply the needs of your child.

What about the child who does not seem to accept responsibility for what he was supposed to do?

Sometimes a child is not overtly disobedient, but he does not seem to take an interest in carrying out tasks that are expected of him. Nothing seems to matter very much to this child, and he seems to lack a sense of responsibility. I suspect he has had a minimal amount of praise for his accomplishments and has been given little opportunity to make his mark on the world.

There is no logical reason for expecting your child to carry out tasks that are expected of him unless there is some inherent reward. Most often this reward lies in your acceptance and recognition of your child's capacity to behave in a way that pleases you. Your child must have some meaningful relationship with you, or there is no inherent reason for his doing things that please you. If his behavior and his reactions are not meaningful to other people, particularly those who discipline him, he will have little or no motivation to please others. He develops a somewhat lethargic and disinterested approach. He has an attitude that "he couldn't care less" what things mean to other people.

Sometimes a child is brought up in a home where his parents, and sometimes servants, do everything for him to please him and minimize the effort of completing the everyday chores. This child is being taught to expect other people to do everything for him. This practice deprives the child of discovering any inherent personal satisfaction in being able to cope by himself. He does not have the chance to find the rewards involved in solving his own problems. As the child reaches adulthood, he is inclined to be demanding. Understandably, he expects things to be taken care of with a minimal effort on his part.

What do I do about irresponsibility?

Give your child small responsibilities and assist him in assuming them. If he is able to handle the responsibilities satisfactorily, the recognition and increased affection you give him in and of themselves reward him and encourage him to take on increasing amounts of responsibility.

I feel you are wise to give your child simple tasks at an early age and reward him for carrying out these tasks. Teach him a sense of pride. Helping a child do things on his own and acknowledging his assistance in family tasks builds a sense of responsibility. For example, most little children around the age of two enjoy doing things that their parents do around the house. Your child may wish to assist in setting the dinner table. If you say you are pleased when your child helps, you will encourage further attempts by your child to help. On the other hand, if you discourage him, ignore him, or are critical of his ability to set the table, you are interfering with his learning a sense of responsibility.

Incidentally, it is of the utmost importance that you yourself demonstrate a sense of responsibility and follow through on it consistently. Absolutely nothing undermines a child's sense of responsibility faster than a parent who abdicates the responsibilities of parenthood by not meeting the needs of his children when they arise or by not assisting his children in mastering the stresses that occur in the life of the growing child.

Does it mean anything if my child always does the opposite of what I ask him to do?

Yes. There is indeed a message behind what your child is doing. He is indirectly asking for your interest. Persistent oppositional behavior is at worst an attempt to get back at you and at best a means of getting attention. Getting back at you is the more direct expression of your child's hostility and resentment. Sometimes a child intentionally and deliberately lies, steals, and is intellectually dishonest, not for the dubious rewards of these actions, but solely to be negative. In general, the child who does this chronically is "crying for attention." Because society frowns upon his actions, the child usually does get your attention, sometimes at the insistence of the police. But your child will accept whatever the consequences are because his actions get him what he wanted most.

Why does my child act this way?

Destructive behavior invariably indicates that something is deeply disturbing your child. The chances are he is desperate. Basically he is frightened and terrified of losing your love.

Negative recognition on your part, while unsatisfactory, is at least some assurance that you care about him. This problem most often occurs in the family of a well-meaning parent who never has enough time to devote some uninterrupted attention to his child. Incidentally, a child in this predicament often bullies other children. He shows great bravado. These overt expressions of strength generally conceal a desperate inner need for someone's love. People generally regard a bully or show-off as obnoxious and want to knock him down a peg or two. It's an unkind reaction. You should remember that the child invariably feels weak to begin with. Knocking him down will simply undermine his already desperate position.

What should I do to help a child who seriously misbehaves?

Once you have recognized how desperate the situation is becoming, it is time for you to tune your antennae to your child's needs and what it may be that is frightening him. Although you are understandably concerned with disciplining your child when he misbehaves, it is absolutely essential that you also focus your attention on what it may be that is bothering him. You have your hands full when a child is misbehaving. Understandably, you have to deal with the trouble at hand and have little time at that moment for coping with the cause of your child's behavior. The best time to discover the cause of his misbehavior—and you will have to work to find it—is between confrontations stemming from your child's bouts of negativism, those times when he is deliberately not doing what you expect of him.

There is one encouraging aspect of this problem. Since your child's behavior usually results from a need for recognition on your part, you yourself can do something about his troubles. He needs attention, recognition, and an attempt on your part to recognize his needs. It's your last chance. Harder than you ever did before, listen to him, pay attention to him, and give of yourself before he turns away from you completely to others who will give him the recognition he craves. These others may not have your set of values, your sense of responsibility, and your basic concern for your child. Remember that in his need for recognition he may do things that are defiant and possibly self-destructive.

Can you give examples?

Yes. Some children create grandiose fantasies and tell about them as if they really occurred. This kind of lying gives a child the emotional satisfaction of feeling that what he is talking about actually occurred. At the same time the lies, if convincing, provoke reactions from the child's friends that help him believe what he is saying. After all, if you tell people stories and they react as if they were true, you begin to believe them yourself. If the lie-becoming-true revolves around the teller doing glorious things or accomplishing great tasks, you can see that this child's self-esteem gets a boost. As adults are inclined to reject someone who lies, you may unthinkingly disregard the emotional satisfactions of the child who lies. Incidentally, the lies themselves and the context in which they are told tell something about the nature of your child's frustrated needs.

Perhaps the most dramatic example is the delinquent, who shows his strength to his friends by actively rejecting standards set by authority figures, including his parents. Sometimes delinquent acts are aimed directly at parents. I have been told by many youngsters in trouble with the police that they stole or burglarized or vandalized simply because they knew it would hurt their parents if they were caught. These children indeed managed to get caught and made their parents suffer. Needless to say, to behave this way a child has to feel very desperate.

What can I do if the situation
gets this bad?

There is very little you can do. At a time like this, *you need help.* Significant or total rebellion is a problem your child will not grow out of. In fact, the chances are that he will grow further into it unless he receives some assistance. The necessary help will invariably involve the concerted efforts of a professional as well as your own. The best thing you can do for your child now is to recognize that he is in trouble and take action by getting him the best professional help you can find.

Chapter XIV

❂❀❂❀❂❀❂❀❂❀❂❀❂❀❂❀❂❀❂

Parental Arguments, Marital Disagreements, and Divorce

Will it harm my child to see me
arguing with my spouse?

I don't think so, but that depends on how you handle the argument. An argument is a normal part of life. It is a disagreement between two people and an attempt on their part to resolve that disagreement. For this reason, having your child witness an argument can be a most beneficial and rewarding experience, provided you explain that "we were sort of angry shouting at each other, but we still love each other." If your child can watch you argue and see that you are still affectionate toward each other, though not necessarily at the same moment, the experience helps your child cope with his own feelings of anger. A child who never sees his parents angry may begin to feel guilty about his own feelings of anger and resentment when they occur, as they surely will. This child may feel that something is wrong with him because he is having feelings that are unacceptable. He may even be overwhelmed by his guilt.

Can an argument go too far?

Absolutely. When an argument includes abusive statements about the people involved, if it leads to objects being destroyed, or if you damage each other physically, the experience can upset your child. It will have little beneficial value and can hardly help your child come to terms with his own anger, since he has just seen you lose control of yours. Moreover, if you engage in such a bout in front of your child, he sees his protectors out of control. His ensuing anxiety is based on his appropriate understanding that he cannot rely on people with such tendencies to protect him. Fears, nightmares, and panic reactions often haunt a child following an episode where parents carry an argument to the point of physical abuse or extensive abusive, degrading remarks aimed at one another.

If I don't want my child to know of disagreements, can I hide them?

You may be able to protect him from the subject involved in the disagreement, but you cannot protect him from knowing about the feelings that accompany your disagreements. When parents believe that it is best not to express anger or annoyance toward one another in front of their children, they carry on their arguments behind closed doors. They hope their child will be unaware of any unpleasantness. However, their subsequent conversation with each other is often accompanied by a coldness and sharpness of tone that tell their child that a deep, intensive hostility is present. When your child notices this, he cannot help wondering about the tension between you. He may have fantasies that are far worse than the realities. Accordingly, I am not in favor of hiding disagreements from your child, since he is capable of *feeling* the tensions that exist. If you persist in hiding them, your child learns to live in a dual world, the real one he feels and the superficial one he pretends to believe in to please his parents. Promoting this type of duality is much worse for your child than hearing you shout at each other now and again.

When should I tell my child
that our disagreements are par-
ticularly serious?

While arguments are to be considered normal, they cannot continue to be considered normal when they' cause a change in the living arrangements between parents. Inform your child that your disagreements are particularly serious when, as a result of an argument, one parent moves into another room or another house, or in some other way creates some form of actual separation. If you tell your child directly that you have argued with your spouse, your child is somewhat prepared if the situation becomes more serious. Your disagreement is easier for your child to understand now than it will be later, particularly if you have hidden the nature of your problem and tended to belittle the intensity of your disagreement. If you try to maintain an atmosphere of "sweetness and light" while a marriage is deteriorating, your child can develop strong feelings of uncertainty about life's events. He may never develop the sensitivity to understand the signs of a deteriorating relationship, and he may even feel that any relationship terminates suddenly and without any warning. If your child can understand, though he may not necessarily accept, that a serious disagreement exists between his parents, he is far better prepared for similar problems if they arise in his own life.

Parents often ask me if this approach is advisable when there is any chance that the marital problem may be resolved so that the parents come back together again in a loving relationship. I feel it is. If you eventually reconcile your differences, you have caused no harm whatsoever to your child by having prepared him for the worst. Better yet, you have given him a vivid example of how a disagreement between people can be worked out for the best.

What shall I tell my child if we decide on a trial separation in the hope of reconciliation?

I think you should tell your child that you have decided to live in different places for a while to see if you can become friends again. Make it clear to him that he did not cause the trouble and that the problem is a problem between his mother and father alone. Emphasize that while living apart you are trying to work out the disagreements so that perhaps you can come back together again as happy as you were in the first place. Your child will accept this explanation, although he won't like it.

How should I handle a separation due to an illness, such as a mental illness or alcoholism?

The best way is to tell your child that your spouse must live apart because he is not well and needs help. If his illness requires hospitalization, your child will more readily understand, since a sick person usually requires the care of a doctor. On the other hand, if the illness or alcoholic condition is not being treated, but is being dealt with by separation of the marital partners in order to decrease the tension between them, your child may have trouble understanding. Often his concern will center around who will take care of the "sick parent," who will feed him, and will see to his needs, and so on. Do *not* let your child get the idea that the sick person has been deliberately abandoned. What is understandable to you as an adult who has tried all possible alternatives without success is incomprehensible to your child. He cannot help feeling that his parent has been abandoned. You must expect to have to reassure him repeatedly that this is not the case.

*What do I tell my child if we
decide to separate permanently
or divorce?*

Your child should be told that every attempt was made to
work out your problems so his "Mommy and Daddy" could
live happily together. Tell him that as it turned out, you felt
you would be happier living apart. Because some children
argue this point and insist that their parents should stay
together, you may have to emphasize that your decision was
made after careful thinking and after trying in every way you
knew how to work matters out. Your child should be helped
to understand, if this is the case, that you both love him and
will continue to see him and take care of him even though he
will spend time with each of you separately.

Do not expect your child to accept the idea of your divorce
without resistance. It will help your child if each of you
attempts to protect the integrity and self-esteem of the other,
so that the child is not faced with the problem of divided
loyalties. But no matter how successful you are in explaining
your separation, the situation will still be difficult for your
child, simply because it will involve a major change in his
living arrangements. He will now have two homes and will
not have the experience of seeing his mother and father interact in either positive or negative ways. These changes alone
will cause your child to feel uncertain.

Some children make the adjustments simply; others find
them extremely difficult. Frequently the child feels resentment, most often for the parent with whom he lives. This
reaction can be very disconcerting to the parent who has
custody of the child. It has been my experience that this
preference occurs simply because your child is inclined to
long for the parent who is not there. He may remember with
great fondness the warmth of that relationship, forgetting the
bad moments. When this reaction is pronounced, it can lead
to disturbed behavior that represents a rebellious attempt to

get back at you for supposedly causing the other parent to go away.

How will my child react to my
telling him we are getting
divorced?

Generally, your child will ask numerous questions about why and what happened. He will focus on the concrete elements of what his future life will be like. Remember that your child may wonder if he caused the divorce. His concern arises in part because children are egocentric and at certain ages feel they themselves have caused most of the events that have taken place in their lives. Your child's concern may also arise because children are commonly discussed as an issue in a divorce and often become the central issue of the dispute between parents. In your child's fantasy he wonders if he might have prevented the separation from happening had he done something differently from the way that he did it. Thus, you must reassure your child that the divorce has taken place because his parents are no longer happy when they live together and are happier being away from each other. Stress that your child himself was *not* the cause, and nothing he could have done would have prevented you from divorcing.

Later, when your divorce has actually taken place, there are many new problems for your child. If, for example, as you begin to develop a social life, your child may think you are bringing strangers into his life to take the place of his "lost" parent, he may resent these friends. Then again, in some instances, your child may accept them simply because he needs to associate with individuals of his absent parent's sex. In either case, you must realize that each person coming into your child's life in this way will be thought of as a replacement for his lost parent. Sometimes this is accepted, and sometimes it is deeply resented. Your child's reaction depends largely on how he feels about the absent parent, not how he feels about the new friend.

I am constantly questioned by divorced parents about possible dangers involved when a child is exposed to a friend who may possibly be your replacement for the parent who is no longer living with your child. The key thing for you to realize is that this situation creates conflict and anxiety for your child simply because he wants to have his original parent back but at the same time he would like to have "someone" to satisfy the unfulfilled needs in his everyday life. What this means, in effect, is that although your child longs for a man (or woman) in the home, accepting a substitute parent is almost the equivalent of severing all ties with his biological parent. You must not underestimate how severe the anxieties of this choice can be. A child frequently has intense emotional reactions and behaves neurotically when he begins to relate to a newcomer who is taking the place of his real parent.

Incidentally, inviting a new companion to sleep overnight can intensify your child's discomfort, since that act represents, quite directly, someone taking the place of your child's lost parent. Since feelings of resentment are quite frequent when this occurs, I think you should exercise great discretion. When you begin to date seriously, your child has to cope not only with the substitute for his "lost parent," but with a parent who is constantly leaving and going off to have fun elsewhere. It may just be too much for your child, who may go so far as to create problems and to be so rebellious that you are forced to increase your attention toward him. Jealousy is very common and can be expected even when your child has a strong relationship with, and need for, a substitute parent.

Will my child resent me for a
broken marriage?

Not necessarily, but your child will have a strong feeling of resentment about a broken marriage, and the person with whom your child has closest contact will most likely be held responsible. If you have custody of your child, that may be you. Your child's resentment occurs even when the other parent has done the bad things that have caused the divorce. Although your child expresses strong feelings of resentment toward you, you must recognize that his feelings result from his frustrated need for both parents to be together. You cannot deal with his feelings rationally by explaining over and over again why the divorce or separation took place. You have to accept your child's feelings and agree that it would have been best for everyone if the marriage had worked out.

What shall I tell my child about his other parent?

Many people are inclined to defend the other parent as a perfectly fine person who was sufficiently different to make it impossible for the marriage to work. This explanation is usually adopted to get your child to show respect for his other parent. While I generally accept this idea, I do not think you should picture your divorced spouse in glowing terms if there is obvious and clear-cut evidence of meanness, rejection, or irresponsibility. Your child will begin to doubt your judgment if you try to support someone who is obviously not worthy. If this is the situation, be as descriptive and realistic as possible in discussing your former spouse. Don't go overboard by degrading the other person or being totally negative. You will upset your child. And you may even be expressing your feelings rather than the realities. Perhaps the best way for me to advise you is to recommend what I would call diplomatic honesty.

Does it adversely affect my child to spend time with one parent and then the other?

For some children it works well. I have seen many children who brag about and seem to enjoy a life with two separate homes, two different rooms, and two sets of toys. On the other hand, I know many children who find it upsetting to have to adjust on separate occasions to two different parents whom they love but have to be with separately. Incidentally, a split-custody arrangement provides some children with more attention than they ever got when their parents were living together. The crucial point is that the effect of spending time with one parent and then the other depends on the amount of direct attention that your child is getting from each parent and the nature of the child's experiences. The alternation itself is neither good nor bad.

Society assumes that children get along better if they live with their mothers than if they live with their fathers. Mothers are supposed to be more geared to the needs of children. While I would be inclined to agree, if a child is under two years old, I question the applicability of this generality to older children. I have known many a divorced mother who resented her children because they limited her own activities. These mothers feel trapped at home and deprived of the various alternatives in the outside world. When a mother feels this way, it seems clear that the child's father may be a far better custodian. Experience supports the theory; I have seen situations in which a child thrives in the custody of his father.

What do I tell my child if a parent abandons him?

Some mothers and fathers have been known simply to pick up and leave a family, never to be heard of again. If this happens to your child, be honest and truthful. Explain that his parent decided to go away and leave the family behind and that you don't know where he (or she) is. As you might suspect, your child may wonder if he caused this to happen. He is sure to be concerned about where his parent is, who is feeding him, whether he is all right, where he sleeps, whether he is thinking of his child, if he misses his family, and whether he will be seen again. It helps to tell your child in the beginning that perhaps his parent was extremely unhappy and had to get away. Ultimately, if no contact takes place, you have to tell your child that this means that the parent does not care enough to want to come back to his family. This interpretation can be very upsetting to your child, but at least it represents an honest evaluation of what the facts are. After all, how long can you go on building up a positive picture of a parent who has left his family and made no attempt to contact it? If you persist for any length of time, your child begins to suspect your judgment.

Is there any difference between
a situation where reconciliation
follows a trial separation and
where an abandoning parent
returns?

Yes. Your child will interpret the situations quite differently. A reconciliation following a trial separation is a successful solution to a problem. Both parents actively participated in a plan whose object was to reconcile differences. Your child will understand this perhaps unpleasant experience as an example of the way in which differences can be successfully resolved. When an abandoning parent returns, a child is happy because a generally unpleasant uncertainty is over and a lost parent has come back. But the child knows there is no more understandable reason for the return than there was for the parent's original decision to depart. In the first instance your child will feel secure in the family. In the second instance your child has absolutely no effective assurance that another abandonment will not occur. After all, no attempt was made to resolve the conflict, and no effort was put forth to reestablish the family structure. He will always somewhere in the back of his mind be afraid that the reasonless abandonment will happen again.

If we have decided to reconcile
and accept marital discord, will
my child have problems?

If there is discord and the communication between marital partners is impaired, your child will be deprived of a family experience where he sees a free flow of conversation, happiness, and cooperative efforts by the father and mother to enhance a family situation. While this deprivation is disturbing to your child, it can sensitize him to the importance of communication between marital partners and can make him more careful about choosing his own spouse. What usually harms the child of an unhappy couple is that his parents are often so focused on their own problems that they do not have either time or energy to be good parents. When the child of a problem marriage gets into trouble, my experience hints that he has not been getting enough attention from his parents.

Incidentally, I believe some children want their parents to divorce; while children rarely tell me so directly, adults who have lived as children in a family where the parents were unhappy and where marital discord prevailed admit they often wished their parents had divorced. But, on the other hand, I have had equal experience with patients whose parents had divorced and who wished that their parents had remained together even if they were unhappy. They most wanted an opportunity to be with both parents at the same time.

What effect will it have on my
child if we would like to get
divorced but cannot?

Your child will be subjected to an environment lacking in happiness, joy, and love as expressed between two adult individuals. Nevertheless, your child may still experience happiness, joy, and love from each of you individually. Children are very adaptable and can probably come to terms with a situation like this if the parents themselves do not use the children as weapons against each other. If you do, your child begins to divide his loyalty and may begin to resent you both equally. Theoretically, a child might find a situation like this much to his liking, since he would be more inclined to get the undivided attention of each parent individually rather than having to share in conversations and events that would be part of "normal" family life. While this aspect of the situation might be beneficial to the child, he is still missing the extremely valuable experience of seeing a male and female expressing warmth, affection, and respect for each other.

*Then you feel the family is
pretty important?*

Absolutely. I think the family is an important social structure because it is the ideal milieu for raising children. Living in a family provides a multitude of experiences that prepare your child for responsibilities that occur later on in life. In fact, I think the family is really much more for children than for the husband and wife. After all, a man or a woman can exist happily alone or together with one another. But a child requires a family environment, a secure home, and friendly consistency. His needs are best provided for within the context of a family.

The family I have in mind has two parents who take a very active interest in their children's emotional well-being as well as in their physical well-being. There are far too many fathers who abdicate this responsibility and turn it entirely over to the mother. There are too many mothers who feel that someone else is equally capable of caring for her children.

I believe that if adults don't want to be parents, they should not have children. Many working mothers use their jobs as an excuse for their unwillingness to assume the responsibilities of motherhood. They tend to downgrade the advantages of motherhood and emphasize the virtues of all other activities. It is my strong conviction that no woman has to have children if she does not want to. But if she decides to have children, I feel it is her responsibility to meet the needs of her children, particularly during the critical early years when no one else can. Too many women belittle themselves by feeling they can turn their children over to someone else who is supposed to be as good as, if not better than, they are. Only their children get hurt.

Some fathers feel their primary responsibility is the support of the family. They become so involved in their work, oftentimes overinvolved to the point where they cannot bring themselves to expend the time and attention that their children need. When this pattern persists over several years, one needs to question whether this father is using his work as an excuse to ignore the responsibilities of fatherhood. In my opinion he is depriving everyone in his family—his wife, his children, and himself.

Chapter XV

Death

*When is my child old enough
to understand the concept of
death?*

Your child will begin using the words *death*, *dead*, *kill*, *died*, and so on, sometime before he understands the meaning of the concept. A child playing with guns may imitate another child by repeating, "I'll kill you—bang!" And sometimes a child will say, "It's your turn to kill me." In such instances, your child is merely using words to describe a play activity. He has no concept of death or killing. Along the same lines, your child may see another child killing ants, beetles, flies, or mosquitoes, and follow suit by stepping on them with equal vigor, without necessarily associating this destruction with death. More specifically, as a general rule your child is not capable of understanding the concept of death before two and a half years of age.

Even then, death usually has meaning to your child only if someone he has known, someone who has "been there" has suddenly gone away. It doesn't make too much difference whether it's an aunt, a dog, or a neighbor. Even when your child is as old as three or four, his awareness of death usually begins one specific day when someone dies. Then your child, for the first time, becomes aware of the concept of death and reacts to it. His reaction is usually a series of questions.

What sort of questions shall I expect?

You can anticipate a series of questions such as: "What does 'died' mean?" "Why can't the doctor fix him up again?" "Where does Aunt Jeanne go when she is dead?" "Where is she now?" "How did she get there?" "Will she come back?" "Can you make him alive again?" "When will you die?" "When will I die?" Sometimes your child's first questions about death will not involve humans. For example, I know one little girl whose queries started with the question, "What's wrong with those plants?" Her father said, "They died." She replied, "I don't want them to die." "Why?" "Because no one can fix them up any more."

Your child's curiosity about death is a difficult problem for you to handle because your child is trying to understand an abstract concept in very concrete terms. He wants to know specific things about death. As you tell him, the answers begin to make him anxious, because all young children in their normally self-centered way are concerned with the topic in relation to themselves. At the same time, parents often deal emotionally with questions about death, simply because they themselves have not come to terms with the problem of death. They become very self-protective in answering a child's questions.

How shall I react to my child's questions about death?

To a large extent, that depends on your own feelings, though I do think you should answer your child's questions, not avoid them. Remember two things: one is your child's wish to know the facts in very concrete terms; the second is your child's feelings. Most young children are initially con-

cerned with the concrete facts. They can't quite comprehend
the idea that someone was able to do things, and all of a
sudden can no longer do things. This change is even more
perplexing when you, who are a figure of great strength and
authority in your child's mind, are unable to restore the dead
person to life. In any child's mind parents possess great
strength. Therefore, you should be able to reverse any event
that takes place. When you cannot, your child feels insecure.

Perhaps it is best for you to describe death to your child
initially by saying that "Uncle Arthur can't do things any
more because he sort of stopped and can't be fixed again.
Even the doctor can't fix him again." Remember to say that
everyone is very unhappy because Uncle Arthur died; everyone will miss him. I think it is highly appropriate to express
grief at this time, particularly if the dead person was someone
to whom you and your child were close. I think it is good for
your child to understand grief and to experience it at an
appropriate time. If your child sees you grieve, it will help
him value life. If you handle death without expressing grief,
you may be telling your child that the dead person was not
only unimportant, but won't even be missed.

You should know that it is also important to express grief
simply because it is a healthy reaction to death. A study was
conducted by a Boston psychiatrist following a disastrous fire
in Boston some years ago. Four hundred people were trapped
in a dance hall and burned to death. The doctor conducting
the study interviewed the families of those people who died.
He found that those individuals who showed the greatest
amount of grief following their loss had fewer physical or psy-
chosomatic reactions later on than those who showed little or
no grief. His conclusion suggests that suppressing a grief
reaction when it is appropriate causes a later manifestation
in some physical disturbance that is, in effect, the equivalent
of the suppressed grief.

It is of the utmost importance that you avoid equating

death with being asleep. Many parents describe death to a child as being "in a long sleep." Understandably, that child begins to fear going off to sleep at night. At best, he may only have nightmares. As a matter of fact, clinical evidence shows quite definitely that sleep disturbances occur when parents describe death in this way.

You must remember that when your child confronts death for the first time he is concerned about the possible death of his own parents. He worries about being left alone. If you are asked, "When will you die?" I think it is appropriate to tell your child that "I won't die for a long, long, long, long . . . long, long, time." Draw out all the "long, longs" to give your child the idea that your death is not planned for the immediate future. Note that you have not denied it will occur. Take the same approach if your child asks if and when he will die. You have to say yes, since this represents one thing we are all sure of, but you can convince your child in his own terms that he will not die for a very, very, very, very long time to come. You cannot expect your child *not* to ruminate about death, no matter what answers you give.

Don't be surprised if your child seems depressed and anxious. He may even cry and say, "But I don't want you to die, and I don't want to die." If your religious beliefs provide for an explanation of life after death, they can guide you in handling your child's questions. But, use these explanations only if you have religion already and your child knows it. Your child will not be comforted and may even regard you with suspicion if you suddenly produce a religious explanation when no religious idea was ever put forth before. It is not quite honest, as your child will sense.

When death enters your child's consciousness, it may be by the death of a pet, perhaps a dog. When this upsetting event occurs, recognize that your child's feelings are no different than if the loss were of a person. Don't simply take the dead pet, throw it in the garbage, and go out and buy another one.

This procedure unerringly conveys the idea that you couldn't care less that your child's pet died. Your child may genuinely benefit by conducting the usual ceremonies of our culture when he deals with the remains of his dead pet. Let your child, if he is so inclined, find a box in which to put the pet. Let him find a peaceful and pretty place to bury it. And let your child place a marker there, perhaps even show an expression of fondness for his dead pet by placing flowers on the grave.

Shall I take my child to a funeral?

The appropriate answer depends on the age of your child and how the funeral is planned. It is also important to consider your child's relationship to the person who has died. If the dead person is in the immediate family, I think it is generally best to bring your child to the funeral. If a young child is to be present at the funeral, I would encourage you to arrange to have the coffin closed to minimize the chance that your child might be subjected to extremes of hysterical reaction. Likewise I would advise that a young child not be present when the coffin is lowered into the ground and covered with earth. If you know the funeral is going to be an extremely emotional event with a great deal of crying and hysteria, perhaps involving people who scream and faint, stay away. Your child, if he is under the age of five or six, will not find this a useful psychological experience, and it may terrify him.

Why go at all?

Experiencing "moderate" amounts of grief is psychologically valuable for your child. I feel this way because I have known many adults who were kept away from the funeral of someone to whom they were close and who live with vivid fantasies. Because they were not allowed to participate, the reality of the funeral never existed. Frequently, their fantasies were far more upsetting than the real experience would have been. I also think it is important for your child to see other people grieving over the loss of someone they have been fond of. While this position may seem inconsistent with my caution about permitting your child to see others in extreme expressions of grief, it is not. Losing someone you like and finding that no one shows any signs of grief is upsetting, too.

Does the death of a parent
create special problems for my
child?

Yes. The death of a parent is a very tragic event for any person. While it is more tragic for a young child who still needs that parent for love and protection, it represents a searing and irreversible loss, no matter how old you are. An excruciating feeling leaves you helpless and makes you question the purpose of life.

Nothing short of returning life to the dead parent can reduce your child's trauma. In short, nothing at all. This fact shapes one part of your child's reaction. Simultaneously, your child will feel anger, particularly a young child, who will feel that the dead parent has abandoned him. Because a child believes that his parents can do anything they want to, a child feels almost as if the dead parent chose to die. No matter how often you in your bereavement explain that this was not the case, down deep your child harbors feelings of anger and resentment. To further complicate things, your child may feel a sense of guilt. Most children have had ambivalent feelings toward their parents at one time or another and may even have wished that a parent would go away or die when, for example, the child was being punished. At certain stages in personality development, a child feels that his wishes can come true. He may very well feel extremely guilty if during that particular stage in his life, a parent actually died. That he should under these circumstances feel guilt is understandable.

As the surviving parent, what shall I tell my child?

Your child's primary concern probably centers on you and your death. Your child fears that he will lose you, too, and will require a great deal of reassurance that this is not necessarily so. If death was the result of an accident, you can expect your child to want you to protect yourself and avoid any activity that might cause you to have an accident. How you reassure your child naturally depends upon what caused the death of the other parent. If death followed an illness, you can reassure your child simply by affirming your good health (if you are in good health).

Whatever the situation, while reassuring your child, I think you should tell him that it will take a long time to get over his unhappy feelings about his parent's death and that in a way he will never, ever, completely get over his feelings of sadness and his missing that person. Also tell your child that no one will ever be able to replace that parent, and that you know it. Unfortunately, many parents handle this situation in quite the opposite way. Attempting to reassure the child they say, "Your father is dead, but pretty soon you'll feel better and get over it." I think it is far wiser to acknowledge your child's feelings and make him feel free to discuss his parent's death. Let him talk to you about his feelings. And remember, you cannot be too generous with reassurance.

How will my child react to the death of his sibling?

One of your child's first concerns if his sibling has died is the fear that he will be next. This fear is based on the fact that a child's ideas occur in a kind of contiguous way. He identifies with an event and sees himself as a participant in that same event. Your child may also feel guilty. Almost every child has some feelings of resentment about his sibling. He may even have had real death wishes toward that sibling. The other child's actual death may be interpreted as the fulfillment of your child's own wish, which can cause severe and debilitating guilt. In fact, the amount of ambivalence and guilt the child feels is almost directly in proportion to the amount of sibling rivalry involved. It is important that you assure your child that nothing he did caused his sibling's death. Furthermore, you can reassure him by telling him that nothing anyone did caused the death and that everyone did as much as possible to keep his sibling from dying.

In this situation, as in the previous ones I have described, I think it is important for your child to share your grief, to understand and recognize your feelings of loss. While some parents are inclined to remove all objects associated with a child who has died, I think it is better to keep a few things to preserve some memories. If you deal with anyone's death as something to be forgotten, your child may get the feeling that life is so unimportant that when a person dies no one even cares, obviously a very threatening concept.

You can have one worse problem, if your child was in some way responsible for the death of his sibling. For example, a patient of mine, when a child, failed to watch a young brother in a wading pool. While she was involved in reading her book, the little boy drowned. Her guilt feelings were so intense and so repeatedly expressed that her parents sent her to a psychotherapist. If such a tragedy occurs, it proves absolutely nothing to add to your child's existing guilt by expressing any blame. He already has more than he can bear. The only thing you can do is to try to love your child in spite of his negligence.

The ravages of being possible for a death are absolutely horrendous for a child. Since any child will be scarred for life in such a situation, no parent should ever allow his child to be put in a position where he might become responsible for a tragedy. The effects are too awful. Your child just simply must not be in a position where he could be directly responsible for anyone's death. Allowing him to so hazard his future is an absolute abdication of parental responsibility. Don't do it.

What shall I tell my child who
is terminally ill?

Do not tell your child that he is going to die. I don't believe any child can actually cope effectively with the knowledge of his impending death in any meaningful or useful way. In fact, I don't think you can say with complete assurance that he is going to die, meaning, as he will interpret it, that he is going to die soon. One of the reasons why doctors try to keep children who are terminally ill alive as long as possible is because they hope that some scientist somewhere is working on some research that might produce knowledge or a medical technique that may save a child's life. What I am saying is that while there is still hope, however faint that hope may be, it is still there. Your child is entitled to it. However, I do think it is only fair to answer your child's questions about his illness. If he expresses a fear that he may die, say, "Yes, you are sick, and it is serious. The doctors and nurses are working hard to make you well so that you can come home soon." Hope is a very important element to use at a time like this.

When I am called in to help care for terminally ill children in hospitals, I advise the doctors, nurses, and parents to engage the child in activities that have a future, projects that may be started today and worked on tomorrow and the next day. I think it helps a child to orient himself to the future. He should not do something that ends today, only to be faced the next day with some other task that has no continuity either with the past or with the future. Quite unconsciously, many parents stop talking with a child about his future, particularly if the child has a long-term, chronic illness that will prevent him from reaching adulthood. This particular child is never asked the question, "What do you want to be when you grow up?"

It is quite common for parents, doctors, and nurses to begin to indulge a child when he is discovered to have a terminal illness. They often stop disciplining the child, give him everything he wants, and begin treating him in a way that is quite different from everything that happened in the past. This reaction is quite understandable in the light of an adult's emotions, but it is unfair to your child. I don't think any child really enjoys these indulgences. More important, they disrupt the natural course of his life and differ sufficiently from his past so that he has to adjust to a totally new set of standards. For this reason, you should be nice, loving, and reassuring, but don't stop using the usual forms of discipline, or in any way alter the techniques or procedures you have used with your child in the past.

Chapter XVI

❖❖❖❖❖❖❖❖❖❖❖❖❖❖

The Child in Trouble

Are all behavioral disturbances
due to emotional problems?

Many are; but not all. Generally speaking, behavioral disturbances can be considered to be caused either by (1) environmental factors or (2) physiological factors. The emotional problems of common parlance are usually those that are attributable to upbringing, to a child's experiences, and to environmental factors in general. Unfortunately, our society has become amateurishly inclined to diagnose all behavioral disturbances as psychological or environmental in origin. That is why you constantly hear such phrases as "A home like his," "What that child has gone through," and "With a father like that." The truth is that many behavioral disturbances are not environmental.

In my practice I have seen many children who have a physiological disorder that, in actual fact, causes their disturbed behavior. Many children sustain some minimal damage to the central nervous system during the time of pregnancy, delivery, or early postpartum state. The delivery process itself causes a certain amount of stress on the baby and a great deal of pressure on the brain, particularly as the infant passes through the birth canal. At this same time the baby, who has relied solely on the oxygen supply from his mother, now has to rely upon his own resources to breathe. As the infant makes this transition, there is sometimes a sufficiently prolonged delay to cause some minor brain damage because of lack of oxygen. Incidentally, it is often very difficult to ascertain whether or not substantial brain damage has taken place until later, sometimes not until the child goes to school and is faced with problems of formal learning. Other physiological causes for behavioral disturbances include hormone imbalances, biochemical imbalances such as changes in the blood-sugar level, and other factors associated with nutritional deficiency. But the most frequent physiological cause for behavioral disturbances is a dysfunction of the nervous system, which includes the brain and all the connecting nerves. Frequently this dysfunction is so subtle that a doctor does not observe it during a normal physical examination. Dysfunction of the nervous system can be caused, among other things, by injuries to the brain or some part of the nervous system, by viruses that cause severe inflammation to various parts of the brain, and by certain chemical imbalances that have a deteriorating effect on brain cells. For example, if an insufficient amount of oxygen reaches the brain, substantial damage to the brain cells may occur, which later causes some behavioral disturbance.

Daily, I work with children who show aggressive behavior, hyperactivity, short attention span in school, learning difficulties, poor handwriting, difficulty getting along with peers, severe temper tantrums. Often these children have a history of some unusual complication during pregnancy and delivery. Some have had a normal pregnancy and delivery but have had severe virus infections that might have caused an extremely high fever, perhaps followed by convulsions, which may have preceded a significant behavioral change. With concurrence from psychological test data, I diagnose these patients as having minimal central-nervous-system dysfunction. Strangely, the physiologically based behavioral disturbance often shows up on psychological examination more readily than it does in a neurological examination. This coincidence greatly concerns me, because I have noticed that many parents feel a sense of guilt if a child shows disturbed behavior. They blame themselves. Then they chance upon some professional who delves sufficiently into their lives and their child's past to find some environmental reason that the professional then announces is the cause of the child's disturbed behavior. I believe these professionals are simply and plainly in error of diagnosis because I think if anyone delves far enough into anyone else's life, he can find sufficient reason to explain any behavioral disturbance on the basis of environmental factors.

Obviously it is extremely important to diagnose the cause of behavioral disturbances as primarily resulting from either environmental factors or physiological factors simply because the treatment required for each is different. Frequently a child who shows disturbed behavior owing to some central-nervous-system dysfunction develops an emotional problem superimposed upon his physiological problem because his disturbed behavior causes other people to dislike him, contributes to his failure in school, or in some other way results in rejection. The child subsequently adjusts to this rejection by developing feelings of inadequacy or insecurity. Obviously, a professional can treat the superimposed emotional problem forever without alleviating the real physiological cause at all. In my opinion, this happens all too frequently. In most instances children with central-nervous-system dysfunction suffer from distractability, poor concentration, short attention span, and hyperactivity. This configuration of symptoms is amenable to treatment with medication simply and effectively. As such, it should be treated by the pediatrician, with assistance from a child neurologist and child psychologist.

I would like to point out here one frequently ignored fact.

Although behavior is the end product of the nervous system, and damage to the brain or nervous system necessarily causes some behavior disturbance, a child who has some dysfunction of the nervous system or brain damage is most definitely not necessarily emotionally disturbed or intellectually limited. On the contrary, many children whom I have diagnosed as having clear-cut brain damage are intellectually gifted and are within the genius level. Moreover, many children who have some damage to the nervous system are happy, contented, and well adjusted. They have learned to cope with nervous-system dysfunction in a way that is not dissimilar to the way a person who has some deformity learns to compensate for his defect. Of course, the extent of the child's adaptation depends on the degree of nervous-system dysfunction.

*How soon will I notice a behav-
ioral disturbance in my child?*

Behavioral disturbances best attributable to environmental factors or to irregularities in a child's relationship to other people manifest themselves very early, at somewhere between four and six months of age. Doctors sometimes notice an infant who cries a strange cry, or an infant may show what doctors consider to be poor muscle tone (callously described as a "floppy baby"). Often these symptoms mean trouble with muscle coordination. But sometimes they correlate with behavior problems that develop later on. An infant who shows no eye-to-eye contact or perhaps poor eye-to-eye contact with other people, a child who tends to regard objects and people similarly, who seems not to differentiate between people and objects such as toys, a baby who spends long periods of time rocking back and forth, exhibiting little awareness of the environment or people, may be suffering from a behavioral disturbance. Some disturbed infants spend long periods of time rocking back and forth in such a way that they seem to "shut out the rest of the world." Sometimes they whine in a constant droning manner without any intense reaction, sometimes even without tears. Strangely enough, some disturbed babies are described as "good babies" because they spend long periods of time without making demands on anyone and show little discomfort or boredom and seem placid, content, and quiet. Some may be infants lacking in any desire to have contact with others. Often a disturbed child has feeding problems and refuses to take food for long periods of time, which may be caused by a disturbance in the mother-child relationship and is easily diagnosed when someone else feeds the child successfully.

While no single one of the symptoms I have mentioned is in itself determinative (for example, many happy babies rock a bit when going off to sleep, and every mother has had a child who, on occasion, won't touch a bite), the persistence of these symptoms is a warning sign that emotional disturbance is present. These symptoms do require your attention, to both your infant child and the cause of the problem. Let me give you an example of how a behavior disturbance begins and what you can do about it if you react soon enough. The one I have selected is perhaps the most common of all. I have referred to it before.

Many parents, during the early part of the first year of a child's life, allow an infant to cry for long periods of time in an attempt to get the child to "cry it out." The parents intend to teach the child that he cannot control them. When parents decide upon this misguided tactic, they usually persist in allowing the child to cry, perhaps day after day, night after night, for long periods of time, until the child has "learned." Then they happily report that their baby has learned not to cry.

The tragic result of this "success" is that the baby has given up on people, since no one answered his cries of distress. He has learned to tune out the world and turn inward. He has developed a mechanism of withdrawing from reality whenever he is faced with stress. It may be for this reason that a baby shows no eye contact with others, shows no particular interest in people in preference to objects, and tends to engage in self-stimulation. While such a baby might look like a "good baby," he has in fact developed a defense mechanism characteristic of the schizophrenic.

If your infant begins to behave like this, it is of the utmost importance that you give him increased stimulation. Heroic efforts must be made to offer him love, affection, and security before he gives up on the world altogether. If this manifestation of disturbed behavior is picked up and treated before eighteen months of age, you are more likely to reverse the development of the schizophrenic withdrawal than if it is allowed to continue beyond that stage of development.

I have repeated this example several times because I am gravely concerned about this process. This particular kind of problem is a very common one, and unfortunately it represents one of the most serious forms of emotional disturbance. A tendency to withdraw from reality, once established, is highly resistant to later treatment and may just be irreversible, regardless of what treatment is adopted. I often wonder what would happen to the incidence of schizophrenia if every —that is, each and every—baby were picked up when he cried.

Does it mean anything if my child is slow to walk and to talk?

Many children show some slowness in their ability to walk and talk, which may represent a problem. More usually it simply represents a lag in development. Some children may be a few months to a year behind in developing these skills without anything being wrong. They seem just to experience a general lag of this time interval throughout the course of their development. Nevertheless, when a delay of more than six months occurs, I think it is reasonable and advisable to consult your pediatrician and possibly a neurologist to see what the causes might be.

Sometimes the developmental lag is due to understimulation. Children who have been brought up in an environment where they are highly restricted or where they are not played with and have had little contact with sounds, sights, movement, and other forms of activity that stimulate the nervous system, tend to show slowness in motor development. Generally, if these children are subjected to increased stimulation, they begin to show dramatic changes in their muscle coordination and their capacity to walk and talk. In my practice I have known many mothers who tend to foster dependency in their children to such a degree that they literally prevent a child from walking. In many instances, mothers may respond to a child's need so quickly that the child is never given a chance to say what he wants. These mothers have not encouraged their children to speak. Stimulation exercises the perceptual apparatus that is used not only to receive information from the environment but to interpret it in such a way that it can be useful to a child. Thus, when development lags, one cannot help wondering if sufficient stimulation was offered to entice the child to learn, that is, to develop.

Having said all that, I would like to caution all parents about comparing their children with other children in regard to the "milestones in development," since all children are different and have somewhat different timetables. Many mothers and fathers who become anxious because of some slowness in development only transmit back to their child their anxiety, which in turn creates a problem for the developing child. In general, many slight lags in development and minor discrepancies seem to straighten themselves out. Don't worry about them. I think it is also important to note that many children may show slow development of their muscle coordination but seem to be intelligent and well developed when it comes to the higher mental faculties that deal with learning, problem solving, and other higher mental functions. Incidentally, often one finds that delays in development are more profound, or *seem* more profound, in the early months and years of life than they do later on. After all, if a child is six months behind his chronological age level and always continues to be six months behind his chronological age level, what difference does it really make when he reaches fourteen and is actually functioning at the thirteen-and-a-half-year level?

What are some of the behavioral disturbances of the child in trouble during the preschool years?

Let me list some of these disturbances, but bear in mind that no one of these in and of itself should be considered to indicate severe behavioral disturbance. However, when a behavioral disturbance occurs persistently, and when a number of them occur concurrently, you should begin to question whether your child is in trouble. For example, nightmares and bed-wetting occur from time to time in most children, but continuous nightmares and frequent bed-wetting after a child is trained often signify some emotional trouble. Other indications of trouble are excessive masturbation, total disregard for parental authority, brutality toward siblings, inability to get along with other children, and determined clinging to parents.

These problems are easy to notice because they are a source of irritation for most parents. However, there are other signs of behavioral disturbances that occur in the preschool child which are not as easily noticeable but may signify even more serious behavioral disturbances. The withdrawn child, who seems to be quiet, obedient, very polite, no trouble to anyone, but who smiles very little, and seems to lack the capacity to have fun, may just be a child who tends to withdraw from others and engage in fantasies that are more gratifying than the real world. Unfortunately, many of these children—who are in real trouble—are looked upon as "good and well-behaved children." They are treated as normal, but, in my experience, are apt to come apart later on in life, particularly during adolescence, when they are overwhelmed by the normal stresses of everyday life. How many times have you read in the newspapers about the young man who was God-fearing, carried a Bible, went to Sunday school every week, never uttered a harsh word to anyone, and then one day went out of control and murdered his parents? What, in fact, occurs is that the child, filled with undischarged hostility, commits an act of destruction. He was told that hostility was bad, but was not taught to channel it in some constructive manner. He stored it up until finally his hostility had to come out. Be aware of the child who is so good that he never shows any anger, hostility, or rebelliousness. He needs help.

If my child shows signs of these emotional problems, what possible causes should I look for?

If you notice one or more of these problems, first rule out the possibility that your child suffers from some physiological disturbance, such as a metabolic disorder or a nervous-system dysfunction. This requires the help of a pediatrician and perhaps a neurologist and a psychologist. Often emotional disturbances occur because there have been recent family arguments and discord. Frequently a child will develop some of these problems when his family has moved from one place to another, an event which disrupts your child's life when he has to give up his friends, find new ones, and adjust to a new community. At times disturbed behavior occurs because your child has been terrorized by another child. Perhaps he has been so terrorized that he has not even told you of his fears.

Conceivably, disturbances could occur following the birth of a sibling. Traumatic happenings in a child's life often result in symptoms of disturbed behavior. What I have in mind is a death in the family, a severe parental threat, a surgical procedure, a frightening event on a television program, and even such things as an injury or severe burn. There are numerous other traumatic events in a child's life, but I don't think I need to list them to make my point.

In dealing with preschool children who have problems, I find that symptoms of disturbed behavior usually occur as a result of some difficulty in parental management. A child may feel rejected or unimportant, or may learn to feel unloved and unprotected through inconsistent handling on the part of his parents. While encountering these problems is always discouraging because of the child's suffering, I am encouraged by the fact that parents can do something to rectify their mismanagement if they wish. That, after all, is why I counsel parents in the course of my work.

What are some of the behavior
disturbances of the child in
trouble when he goes to school?

The major behavioral disturbances of the child in trouble in school center around learning disabilities. A child may show a poor attention span, have difficulty concentrating, or encounter problems learning to read or to write. Some children show defiant behavior, rebelliousness, and an unwillingnes to do what the teacher requests. In each case, the child may be rejected by the teachers. The learning disabilities and the behavioral disturbances often cause the child to be subjected to greater pressure than a well-behaved child, and feelings of inadequacy result, which in turn increase the rebelliousness, which in turn increases the pressure—a vicious cycle. Strangely enough, disturbed school behavior occurs much more frequently in boys than it does in girls. In fact, school disturbances are substantially more common in boys than they are in girls.

Frequently a schoolchild's disturbed behavior is caused by some minor neurological dysfunction and is not initially evidence of an emotional conflict. His learning disabilities stem from minor brain damage. Or perhaps he has a short attention span, which may be based on difficulty controlling his impulses because of some minor neurological dysfunction. If these problems go unrecognized, which happens frequently, or are not treated by administering appropriate medicines, a child may, as I have already pointed out, develop an emotional problem superimposed upon his physiological difficulties. These secondary problems are not too different from primary emotional problems, which are themselves all too common.

Many schoolchildren who are in trouble show a reluctance to go to school. They discover all kinds of excuses to avoid going. Some develop a "school phobia," a fear of going to school, which is not to be confused with a reluctance to go to school. This phobia is often rooted in a disturbed parent-child relationship. The child is reluctant to leave his parents and his home to go into an unknown environment without the protection of his parents. When there is tension at home, many children are fearful while they are in school because they are worried about what is happening at home. They are afraid that they will return home to a situation of some acrimony, possibly one that is explosive. When a child is preoccupied with these fears, quite naturally he shows difficulty concentrating. I have found, incidentally, that many children who show behavior disturbances in school are reacting to both the parents working. If a child is—or feels—neglected and is not getting enough attention, he may learn that he can at least get negative attention if he prevents his parent from going off to work by creating problems at school. This behavior serves the child's purpose of gaining the parent's attention and at the same time punishing him for neglect. All too often, there is justice in the child's reaction.

Another manifestation of a behavioral disturbance is bullying other children. Children rarely bully unless they have some underlying fear, particularly a feeling of inadequacy. Young bullies are making an attempt to reassure themselves about the feeling of strength that they do not basically have.

I want to emphasize another very important point that is frequently ignored. Sometimes teachers are frightening to children, and sometimes the school adopts forms of punishment, institutes methods of discipline, or makes demands upon a child that are terribly frightening and threatening. Your child's reaction is a proper, normal reluctance to go to school. Look into these possibilities before even considering that your child suffers from a learning disability or an emotional disturbance. While I don't mean to be overly critical of schools, I do mean that any child who seeks to avoid going to school may simply be having a reaction or possibly an over-reaction to some event which took place in the school or to some person associated with the school. On numerous occasions I have treated a child whose behavior includes sporadic episodes of unwillingness to go to school. The behavior has perplexed both the school and the child's parents. On further inquiry, and after talking alone with the child, I have discovered that he has become fearful of a particular bully who has threatened him. Primed and ready to deal with a major emotional problem, I was most pleasantly surprised to find that the child's problems subsided when the bully was told to stop bullying.

What other problems are encountered after adjustment to school and before adolescence?

During this particular time in a child's life, the major problems encountered are those of truancy from school, delinquent behavior, rebelliousness, and confrontations with the law.

Stealing is common at this time. Generally, delinquent behavior, including wanton destruction, defacing buildings, and harassing strangers, represents a child's desire for attention. That the attention he gets will be negative usually means he has received no positive attention, which usually means his parents neglect him. In an indirect way, the child may be crying out for help. When treating youngsters who have been wildly delinquent, I have often found that their delinquency is directed against a neglecting father or, alternatively, a father who is so overbearing that his child never seems to be able to approach his expectations and get his respect and admiration. In either case, the father is unapproachable. The child's delinquent act represents an attempt on his part to get through to his father, to penetrate his attention barrier, even if the child brings punishment on himself and embarrasses his father publicly.

Stealing, while it can represent delinquent behavior, is also a very common misguided adventure. When it occurs, it usually occurs on infrequent occasions. Often this type of stealing is encouraged by friends and in a child's mind does not represent greedy acquisitiveness as much as it represents conformity to group pressure. Thus, if you discover your child has stolen, your reaction can to a large extent determine your child's reaction and his subsequent concept of himself. He can be someone who has unwittingly fallen into committing a "misdeed" or he can be a certified, seasoned criminal with no hope for future rehabilitation. To avoid the latter image, I usually urge parents to react to an initial stealing episode with great concern but not with excessive punishment. In such a case, do not label your child as a crook and show continued mistrust of everything he does. If you do, you will only destroy your child's sense of self-esteem and give him the impression that you expect him to continue his misbehavior. He may unconsciously comply with your fears and/or wishes.

Sometimes a child will engage in stealing in an attempt to acquire objects that he can use as little bribes or that he can offer as "deals on the side" to gain acceptance by his class-mates. Stealing for this purpose occurs most frequently among children who never seem to be able to win in competition with their peers. They lack self-esteem and are not highly regarded. When they are unable to follow the rules of the game and gain acceptance that way, they try bribery. Inci-dentally, a child may have learned this behavior from a parent who gives a present as a reward for acceptable behavior.

There are some adults who, regardless of their social status and lack of real need for material objects, find themselves compelled to steal. These people are, in a way, attempting to satisfy some unconscious wish or need. They find them-selves driven to shoplift and seem to gain a great satisfaction from the adventure involved in stealing. It is as if the effect of tempting danger is their primary need. These adults and the adolescent who steals are engaged in behavior that has similar causes. Some, by trying to seek punishment, are trying to expiate guilt for something they feel they have done wrong. Others are looking for excitement that they can get only by tempting danger. Others are in some way trying to punish the authority figures in their lives. All are mixed up and need pro-fessional help.

What causes later disturbed behavior?

Later disturbed behavior is essentially caused by the same problems found at previous levels of development. The prob-lems simply become apparent later. Unfortunately, the chances are that you missed noticing the problem earlier in your child's life. On the other hand, if there really was no earlier behavior disturbance, the trouble may appear when your child is older because his environment has changed. His opportunities for manifesting disturbed behavior did not arise until environmental conditions were right. An example of this latter possibility is delinquent behavior that begins when a child moves to a new community. Before the move there were no signs of emotional problems. Then, because the child is in a new community, perhaps subjected to a new group of friends who are pressuring him, his previously suppressed wishes to punish his parents have their first opportunity to express themselves. Delinquent behavior, stemming from unresolved emotional problems, results on a grand scale.

Do you feel I should get pro-
fessional help when my child is
in trouble?

Yes. Too many parents try to go it alone, or worse, selfishly deny that a problem exists. Thus, while I think it is important for you to make some attempt to deal with your child's problems, it is better to have a third person, usually a professional, involved in solving the problem. When a child discusses his problems openly with you, talking confidentially about ideas and feelings about which he himself feels ambivalent, he usually finds that the discussions interfere with your continuing relationship. Speaking to a "third person" gives your child a sense of freedom that helps him express his real feelings. Hopefully, this third person has no direct influence on your child's life. His uninvolved impartiality helps maintain the air of confidentiality that gives your child the best chance to talk about his feelings and perhaps gain some insight into his own motives. Moreover, the uninvolved professional, not being directly involved in your child's life, is relatively objective and can point out elements that you as parents might possibly not see.

When you look for a professional to help your emotionally troubled child, try to find someone whose reputation comes from success in dealing with emotional problems. Look for someone who is practical, empathic, flexible, and common-sensible. Be absolutely sure that his approach is to fit the treatment to the patient's problem, and not the patient to his own unique form of treatment. Remember that the credentials of a professional, while they are important, do not necessarily make for competence. Degrees, titles, lectures on subjects that pertain to your child's problem, even the authorship of several books—these are not the equivalent of success in coping with the kinds of problems you are faced with. Ending up with the wrong professional can be a disaster.

What harm can an incompetent professional do?

Sometimes an incompetent professional will treat a problem that doesn't exist. I can think of no situation that is worse, except perhaps to deny treatment to a person who really has a problem. By treating a problem that doesn't exist, the professional may positively create one. I have often heard it said that "some treatment is better than no treatment." I disagree completely. Professionals should not engage in treatment that is unnecessary, because the treatment stigmatizes the child and often greatly disrupts his everyday life.

I have seen many professionals who take a child into treatment simply because he seems to lack motivation, is "low-keyed," and not competitive. The child may be contemplative, quiet, and prefer to engage in intellectual activities rather than physical activities. I have known many "qualified" professionals who see this behavior as a problem when, upon careful examination, the child simply has these characteristics. His behavior is quite normally caused by his temperament. Incidentally, this particular "problem" is sometimes precipitated by a school that may prefer to have a keyed-up child who is extremely competitive.

Youngsters who are extremely hyperactive with short attention spans are looked upon as anxious and emotionally disturbed. A routine psychological examination locates symptoms of some emotional disturbance. They undergo a prolonged course of intensive psychotherapy in an attempt to help them "work out" their supposed hostility and aggressiveness. The psychotherapy is unsuccessful. On careful physical and neurological reexamination many of these same children are found to have neurological disturbances. Treatment geared to the physiological defect is completely effective in a relatively short period of time.

In my opinion, unnecessary psychotherapy is the most harmful treatment. When a youngster with a physiological disturbance or no disturbance at all is treated psychotherapeutically, he feels stigmatized and inadequate. The treatment takes him out of the mainstream of his life. The hours he spends talking to a therapist could be spent with his friends, playing and learning. His parents suffer, emotionally and financially. They become introspective and wonder where they went wrong. Their newly created guilt is "fed back" to their child, which tends to enhance the development of an emotional problem. Ultimately, if the psychotherapy is extended, the child indeed does develop an emotional problem. What a way to solve a problem!

If a child absolutely needs psychotherapy, treatment should definitely be initiated. But psychotherapeutic treatment for children should be as direct and as short-term as possible. Long-term, intensive psychotherapy requiring as much as three sessions a week over a period of years interferes sufficiently with any child's free time and his interaction with other children so that treatment itself can create a problem unless it is desperately essential to the child's emotional needs. Every professional should realize that it is imperative for children to get back into childhood as quickly as possible. After all, childhood is a crucial period in development upon which later personality is based. Psychotherapeutic treatment is not.

What allows professionals treat-
ing children to go astray?

Society has only recently fully recognized the importance of psychology and psychiatry. Psychologists and psychiatrists, once ridiculed and denigrated, are erroneously credited with miraculous powers of cure. The pendulum has swung. They are lionized nowadays; no matter how minor the emotional disturbance, the psychologist is called in immediately. He is fully licensed to locate the problem causing the behavioral disturbance. Everyone expects him to, and he obliges by trying his hardest.

What happens if things are going to go wrong is this: the doctor wants to cure his patient. He works hard to help. But if any professional looks hard enough at anyone, even at you or me, he cannot avoid eventually finding substantial reasons for attributing the alleged emotional disturbance to something in the patient's environment or experience, and he makes a diagnosis. The "problem," once located, calls for full-blown treatment, which is initiated. The hitch is that the "problem" located by the professional is not the "problem" causing the disturbance. Understandably, the psychotherapy fails dismally. The example of the neurologically damaged "problem" child who fails to respond to treatment is all the example needed.

Erroneous diagnosis is always bad. The unnecessary treatment that results is always unnecessary. Overall, the only way to minimize unnecessary treatment is for society to recognize the most frustrating fact of all: There are some emotional problems that even the most competent psychologist or psychiatrist cannot and should not treat.

What do you mean?

From time to time I am asked to help emotionally troubled children with behavioral disturbances whose problems I diagnose as untreatable or, at best, highly resistant to treatment. This situation perplexes and frustrates any professional, myself included, since each of us would like to feel and be sufficiently powerful to cure any possible problem for any patient. Nevertheless, doctors and society in general must recognize that there are some problems that a patient simply must learn to live with. Why? Because to treat the emotional problem is more disruptive for the troubled patient than for him to learn to cope with the problem directly. Acknowledging the limits of treatment hurts the unscrupulous professional in the pocket-book; it hurts the most professional professional in the ego. Let me give you an example.

Recently I was called in to see a youngster who had contracted a blood disease that required hormone injections for him to survive. The little boy, aged five, was given high daily doses of male hormones. He became aggressive, his voice took on a deep tone, hair grew on his face, and he showed many of the other characteristics of a normal adolescent. In particular, he began to show sexual interests, demanding to be cuddled by the nurses who cared for him. Perhaps incidentally but yet significantly, the hormones that were administered caused the boy's penis to become rather large. The youngster was confused, the staff was perplexed, and other patients to whom he exposed himself were curious. Overall, the boy's behavior somewhat overwhelmed the doctors and nurses who had to handle him, since they could not recognize that he was still a young child who happened to have many adult physical characteristics. They were inclined, consciously and unconsciously, to react to him as an immature adolescent, not as a young child who was artificially (as part of his treatment) afflicted with certain adolescent secondary sex characteristics. As hard as it was for the doctors and nurses to care for him, it was even more difficult for the boy to cope with his own impulses and particularly with the feedback he got from other people. He was totally confused.

The doctors and nurses were ready to try anything. They wanted a psychological explanation for the boy's behavior, and they wanted me to get the child to behave normally. I told them I couldn't help because the hormones were causing the abnormal behavior, not emotional disturbances. They must either stop the daily hormone injections or live with the abnormal behavior.

A more sophisticated example involves a twelve-year-old girl who had had a brain tumor removed one week before I first saw her. She complained of severe headaches and showed excessive clinging behavior. She was extremely demanding toward her mother. At times the girl responded to voices and people not apparent to others. These visions particularly distressed the doctors and nurses who had to care for the girl, so they referred her to me. Although the girl's mother had clearly been inconsistent in handling her in the past, I had to consider that the disturbed behavior might be a reaction to her brain tumor, her operation, and the unpleasantnesses of the postoperative period. I felt it was best to tolerate her disturbed behavior, offering her simple reassurance until she was sufficiently recovered for me to evaluate the true nature of her emotional problem. I declined to initiate psychotherapy. As it turned out, the girl's behavior returned to what was described by her mother as "normal." True, "normal" included behavior I might have characterized as demanding and clinging. But neither the mother nor the daughter felt any particular concern. Apparently I had been wise to consider that the girl had experienced a severely traumatic surgical procedure. I was correct in deciding to leave her behavior problem alone rather than push this youngster into intensive psychotherapeutic sessions. She was having enough trouble as it was, without having to cope with a professional. Incidentally, you too must accept the fact that your child will have problems that you cannot help him with.

Can I do anything to help my child accept the problems he must live with?

Yes. You can recognize, and help him recognize, that problems are relative. A child who lives on hormone shots that make him behave strangely is better off than a dying child. It is easier for your child to live with problems if he accepts them as a normal part of normal life. In fact, problem-solving adds zest to life. Of course, it helps your child to know that you want to help with his problems. You should let your child know that you care about him, that you will be there to help him when he needs you. Make him understand that his feelings concern you, that you enjoy him as he is, together with his problems. In short, that you love him as he is. Believe me, when your child sees you expressing love like this, he will learn from you to love. After all, didn't you learn to live with some of your problems? And, in spite of them, don't you give and receive love? To look at it another way, who wants to know the perfect human being? Or, worse yet, to be the perfect human being? It would be a terrible responsibility, and it would be absolutely impossible to find anyone who could love you.

Index

Index